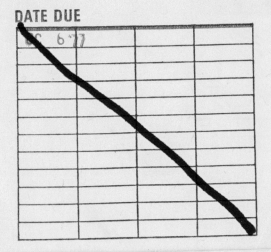

THE TEACHING-LEARNING PROCESS

THE
TEACHING-LEARNING
PROCESS

JAMES L. KUETHE

Johns Hopkins University

KEYSTONES OF EDUCATION SERIES

ACADEMIC EDITORS

MERLE L. BORROWMAN, *University of Wisconsin*
ROBERT J. SCHAEFER, *Teachers College, Columbia University*
ISRAEL SCHEFFLER, *Harvard University*
EDWARD JOSEPH SHOBEN, JR., *American Council on Education*

SCOTT, FORESMAN AND COMPANY

To My Mother and Father

TABLE OF CONTENTS

AN OVERVIEW OF THE PROCESS
The Concepts of Teaching and Learning
Participants in the Teaching-Learning Process
The Study of the Teaching-Learning Process

LEARNING: THEORETICAL CONSIDERATIONS
Connectionist Learning Theories
Other Controversies
Theoretical Controversy and Classroom Practice

STRUCTURING A DISCIPLINE OF EDUCATION
Classroom Hypotheses
Problems with Empirical Research
The Development of Educational Principles
A Model for Forming Research Hypotheses in Education

SOME EMPIRICAL ASPECTS OF TEACHING AND LEARNING IN THE CLASSROOM
The Dynamics of Classroom Learning
Reinforcement for Learning in the Classroom
Reinforcement and the Maintenance of Behavior
Reinforcement Schedules and Extinction
Forgetting
The Distortion of Recall by Values and Predispositions
Selective Recall

PREFACE

Educators and laymen alike, in discussing problems in contemporary and historical education, frequently use words such as *teaching, learning, intelligence, motivation, and creativity.* Analysis reveals that many of the arguments that arise from such discussion result not so much from real differences of opinion as from more subtle discrepancies in the definition of these basic terms—discrepancies which are frequently not made explicit.

The Teaching-Learning Process will make the reader aware of these problems of definition, and will seek to adopt a working definition of each of the critical terms so that disagreements may represent real differences of opinion rather than misinterpretations of what is said.

Besides defining the basic language of education, the book probes deeply such fundamental ideas as reinforcement, retention and forgetting, transfer of learning, and basic needs of the student. It shows how educational principles can be derived by viewing empirical principles of learning in the light of established educational values.

The emphasis throughout the book is on the individual student. The determinants of his attitudes and motivations are discussed, and the prospective teacher discovers how he can shape these attitudes and use the motivations of the student to help that student reach both immediate and distant goals.

Finally, this book discusses *specific* teaching methods, traditional as well as new, in a manner which emphasizes flexibility in choosing among them to meet the requirements of individual students and specific learning situations.

•

An Overview

of

the Process

•

THE CONCEPTS OF TEACHING AND LEARNING

Responsibility for the continuity of the culture of complex modern societies has not been left to chance but has been given to formal institutions, the schools. For a long time very few people other than educators expressed active concern about the methods and results of the education enterprise. Parents were often satisfied by the fact that their children were occupied most of the day, and employers were happy as long as they could find people who had acquired the special skills needed by their particular business.

What was once an area of public apathy has become a topic of concern to everyone—a concern so important that it often arouses emotions bordering on hysteria. Whether one points to Sputnik or more involved social forces as the cause of this interest, a pervasive and deep concern about education now exists. Modern communication methods, particularly the mass media, have transmitted the anxieties of the more outspoken into every home. Many people who otherwise would never have considered the importance of education are constantly informed of the critical role of the schools in the national economy and in national defense. They are also told of the increasing difficulty of finding qualified teachers, and they begin to wonder whether or not *their* child is receiving his just share of what the schools have to offer.

Increased concern has produced many consequences, some desirable and some less fortunate. One negative result has been the unreasonable pressure to achieve placed on both students and teacher. On the other hand, there have been many innovations in curriculum, teacher training, and other aspects of education which should benefit the student, and the status and financial remuneration of educators have risen. Furthermore, questions of who should teach, what should be taught, and how it should be taught are constantly being raised. And this is as it should be. The value of raising a meaningful question is in marked contrast to the dangers of trying to impose a dogmatic answer to the problems of education. The man who raises a significant social question deserves respect and praise, but the man who insists that he has the answer must be regarded with suspicion. The consequences of a wrong decision may be subtle, and there is no guarantee that the mistake will be detected before considerable harm has occurred.

It is our task to study what is known about the teaching-learning process, not in order to formulate mandates, but rather to seek guides and explore the possibilities that one practice will produce better results than another. An important consideration will be the values that so clearly separate the discipline of education from the traditional social sciences. First, an overview of the teaching-learning process and an introduction to the significant participants.

TEACHING DEFINED

For the purpose of discussion we shall define teaching quite broadly as causing people to learn. This is essentially the same as the dictionary definition of *teach* which uses phrases like "to make to know how," "to impart the knowledge of," and "to make aware by information, experience, or the like."

Some educators use the word *teach* in a different way. They use the word to describe the activity of a teacher regardless of whether the students learn as the result of this activity. This use of the word *teach* is similar to the modern use of the word *sell* when a man says, "I was out selling all day but no one bought anything." To use the word *teach* in this way is, if not wrong, at least confusing. If I say that I taught my son to swim, there is the strong implication that he learned to do so. The context makes the difference. By this definition, "He teaches French" does not require that anyone learn, but "He taught French to them" or "He taught them French" does seem to imply that learning occurred.

Our original definition (to teach is to cause learning) not only is in agreement with the dictionary but has the same meaning in different contexts. This meaning is not new. William Heard Kilpatrick said, "We haven't taught, till the child has learned."[1] Later John Dewey compared teaching and selling:

> We should ridicule a merchant who said that he had sold a great many goods although no one had bought any. But perhaps there are teachers who think they have done a good day's teaching irrespective of what pupils have learned. There is the same exact equation between teaching and learning that there is between buying and selling.[2]

Teaching includes having people read certain material, see particular demonstrations, and engage in various activities as long as learning is one of the products. Naturally our definition includes the popular concept of teaching—the standard teacher-student interaction in which learning is the main product. Essentially, a teacher guides the activities of a student in order to produce learning. This guidance may be indirect, as when a student is told to read a particular book, or even less structured, as when a student is told "Read anything you can find on the agricultural practices of the Incas." At the other extreme is highly structured and continuously directed teaching. In a spelling drill, for example, the teacher constantly guides the learning of students on a highly structured task. (See Figure 1.)

The process of teaching and learning varies along other dimensions besides extent of structure and extent of teacher monitoring. Other variables are the extent of the student's awareness of what he is to learn, the extent of measurement, and the extent of feedback, all of which are closely related. Even when a student is writing an essay at home on the topic of his choice, he knows that he will be graded on spelling, grammar, and aptness of thought. He knows, then, what facts and skills he is supposed to have acquired. The teacher has assigned the essay in order to estimate the extent of the student's learning. Besides being a measure of learning, the essay exercise will also lead to some further learning when it is graded by the teacher and the student receives this feedback. Unfortunately, there is usually a lamentable delay between performance and knowledge of the adequacy of the performance, i.e., feedback.

A different situation exists when the student is set the task of learning to spell certain words or mastering a French-English vocabulary. Perhaps he will produce nothing concrete, analogous to the essay, which the teacher can rate. However, the student

FIGURE 1. *Teaching-Learning Activities as a Function of Extent of Teacher Monitoring and Extent of Structure of the Learning Task*

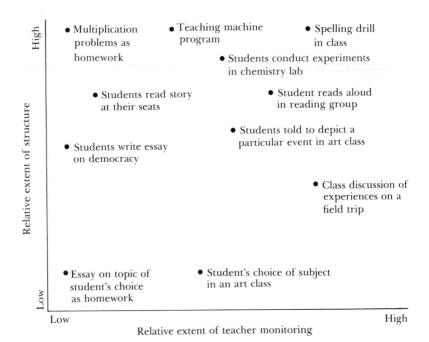

knows his task, his goal, is *to learn*. If he has been told to learn to spell the words on the week's spelling list, he knows exactly what to learn. When the assignment is to read Chapter 6 of his history book, he is often not sure exactly what he should learn, but he does know that he is supposed to learn something. In most school-related performance, the student knows his task is to learn something. In this way formal education differs from the rest of an individual's life experience. Outside of the schools, *learning is a by-product.*

Learning, outside of the schools, is usually a by-product of a person's efforts to reach a desired goal or of his taking part in a desired activity. Normally the person's goal is not *to learn*, but to reach the state of having acquired certain skills or goals. For example, regardless of what I may say, I do not want *to learn* Spanish; rather, I want to be able *to speak* Spanish. If, like an engineer working on the Tower of Babel, I could suddenly acquire a new language, I would be quite willing to forgo learning it. Often we hear a student protest, "Why should I learn that? What good is it going to do me?" Or, "I am going to be an engineer; why am I required to take history and learn a lot of dates?" We hope the student is wrong about the way the history course is taught, but the point remains that the student sees that his task is *to learn* and knows that he will be graded on how much he learns.

The attitude of the student is not by any means unwarranted when we consider how often people are directed to learn material that in all likelihood will not be remembered for very long. Some individuals are instructed to learn the valences of the elements in eleventh-grade chemistry, and these are fairly well forgotten by the time he finishes high school. In the first or second year of college the student takes chemistry again and relearns this material. By the end of college, when the student is awarded his degree in Romance languages, he has forgotten the valences of carbon and oxygen for a second time. We might say that this is all right because no one will ever know the difference—and it is true they will not—but consider the hours of study and instruction that have gone down the academic drain into the sea of unrelated and unremembered facts. It would be interesting to pursue this line of thought, but it is not our intention to study curriculum values.

PROBLEMS WITH A DEFINITION OF LEARNING

Let us take a moment to recapitulate. We have defined teaching as causing people to learn. The teacher, then, would be an individual who causes other individuals—students—to learn. Obviously the nature of learning is a critical part of the understanding of teaching. It would seem that a definition of learning is all that is needed to complete our description of the teaching-learning process, but the task is not so simple. First, it is difficult to define learning in ways that are completely satisfactory. The problem is not dissimilar to that of the biologist if he is pressed to define *life*. Any given definition seems to exclude some elements that we wish to include and fails to rule out other cases that we do not want to admit. Adding to the problem is the practical consideration that we want a definition that is not so technical and qualified as to be unusable.

A prevalent definition of learning is that it is the process by which behavior changes as a result of experience. What problems arise with this definition? Some changes in behavior that result from experience are clearly not examples of learning. If a person twists his ankle, his behavior changes as a result of this experience; he limps. An immediate response to this example might be to say, "Well, everyone knows that is not learning." If it is this easy to find such an obvious problem with the definition, there may be much more subtle difficulties. In this case the definition includes something that is not desirable. It is as if a biologist defined life as things that had the property of growth and then had someone point out that salt crystals grow.

Qualifying the definition of learning by specifying the *types* of experiences that lead to changes in behavior does not seem to help too much; in fact, this is likely to compound the problem. It might be tempting to define learning as changes in behavior that are the result of nonpathological or nontraumatic experiences, but that would exclude the development of neurotic behavior which is pathological and often has traumatic experiences as part of its etiology. Even if the definition limits learning to changes in the central nervous system, the problem remains of alterations in behavior due to organic defects.

So far we have been considering problems that arise from the "result of experience" part of the definition of learning. The "change in behavior" aspect of the definition is even more tricky. There is no way to tell that learning has occurred until some change in behavior is observed. There is no way to measure learning directly: it can only be measured through performance. The teacher gives a test to "measure what the students have learned," but actually the performance on the test is used to *infer* that certain learning has taken place. It is interesting to compare the indirect measurement of learning with the measurement of temperature—also an indirect measurement. When a person consults a thermometer in order to check on the weather, he looks not at the temperature but at the length of a column of mercury that bears a known relationship to other phenomena. He is not really interested in how many inches high the mercury has gone but in whether he should wear a coat when he goes outside. Even though the height of the mercury is an indirect measure, it gives a very close prediction (if the thermometer is accurate) as to how one will feel once out on the street.

Unfortunately, performance as a measure of learning is often more misleading than is the thermometer as a predictor of comfort. For example, most people have had the experience of being so anxious during an examination that their performance suffered. As a result of the stress they were unable to demonstrate what they had learned. If some individuals consistently react to tests with situational anxiety, their level of learning will be consistently underrated. There are, then, personality factors that interact with performance and lower the validity of performance as a measure of learning in some situations. In another situation, perhaps in talking with friends, these same individuals, now relaxed, may reveal by their performance that they had in fact learned.

People differ in their motivation to perform at a certain level or under certain circumstances. At times researchers have made serious mistakes by ignoring the distinction between learning and performance. Attempts to compare the learning capacity of the aged with that of young students have often produced lower "learning" scores for the older people. As has been discussed, performance, not learning, provides the actual data of any study of learning. If the older people were less motivated, they may have found the experimental tasks uninteresting and, as might be expected, not performed as well. However, this would in no way be a reflection of their capacity to learn.

Also, individuals have different systematic ways of responding, called *response sets*, that prevent their performance from being a pure measure of learning. Some work for speed, while others tend to concentrate on accuracy. The way some students study favors performance on objective, multiple-choice, and true-false tests rather than on essay tests. Other response sets favor the tendency to choose "true" instead of "false" on that form of test and to choose the first alternative on multiple-choice tests.

In summary, it can be seen that the examination given by the teacher to measure learning actually produces a performance which represents the interaction of learning with motivation, personality factors, response sets, and other situational factors, including the accuracy of the measuring instrument employed.

The discussion thus far has emphasized that performance may be *lowered* by factors not related to learning. However, in some cases the performance may be *raised* by factors unrelated to learning. When a student on a multiple-choice test circles 1066 as the date of the Battle of Hastings, his performance would seem to indicate that he has learned the lesson. But again, the situation is not quite that simple. It would appear that he can *recognize* the right answer, but could he have *recalled* the date if he were given no choices? Studies have shown that an individual can often identify an answer as right or wrong, even though he is unable to generate the response himself.

Different ways of measuring learning produce different results. Even when performance definitely reflects learning, the learning may be very specific to the particular form of performance. This raises problems of criteria: What level of performance is needed to safely make inferences about what has been *learned?* Another related problem, which will be considered later, is the question of retention: Are the changes in performance transitory or relatively enduring? A third question of fundamental importance to education is—Has the student learned anything he can use in any meaningful way outside of the classroom? This is the seldom measured but central assumption of formal education. The assumption is probably warranted in the case of some classroom learning, e.g., reading skills, but is without doubt in error with respect to some other aspects of classroom instruction. This concern will be given further consideration when we discuss the phenomenon of the transfer of learning. We will ask: To what extent can the individual make use of what he has learned in some past situation when he must cope with some present problem?

So far the discussion of learning has been based on the learning of specific facts and principles, which is, as it should be, the major purpose of classroom activities. But there is another very important area of learning—that of attitude formation. It would not be difficult to argue that the attitude learning that takes place in the classroom is as important as the content learning, especially in the early years of schooling. At the macro level is the formation of attitudes toward education and the schools. If a student finds his school experiences unpleasant and unrewarding, he will often drop out of school as soon as the law permits, or he may complete high school but decide against attending college. Drop-outs are not all dull students for whom learning is a slow, tedious process; the gifted drop-out is prevalent enough to be of concern to many educators and to others who are appalled at this waste of the nation's greatest resource—people of ability. For these individuals, some failure in the teaching-learning process led to the formation of negative, instead of positive, attitudes toward education.

Often individuals learn negative attitudes toward specific school subjects. Mathematics has a poor record on this score, perhaps because it is more difficult to teach successfully than many other subjects. As adults, many people protest that they "block" and cannot think when arithmetic is required. Negative attitudes can develop quickly in learning mathematics because if a person gets "lost," he tends to stay confused. The logical dependence of each step on the last in mathematics is in contrast to some other subjects where it is possible to be perplexed about one topic but fully understand the next. Also, mistakes are more obvious in a discipline based on quantification rather than on qualification. In subjects other than mathematics it is possible to have the satisfaction of being partly right. Perhaps some teachers of arithmetic have been wrong in denying students these partial rewards.

The learning of attitudes is important not only for the future orientation of the student but also for his current motivation to learn. There is a cumulative interaction between attitudes and classroom performance. Negative attitudes lead to inferior performance which in turn produces additional frustration and strengthens negative attitudes.

In addition to *content* learning and *attitudes* toward learning and education is the *social* learning that takes place in the classroom. As a result of participating in the interpersonal relations that are a part of the classroom experience, the student learns about people—the many ways in which they are alike and the many ways in which they are different. He develops social expectations that allow him to predict how others will react in a particular situation and how they will react to him if he behaves one way rather than another. He develops plans, or concepts, about the relationships that exist between people. The importance of the social concepts developed early in life and through the school experience is obvious and does not require elaboration at this point.

AN EMPIRICAL APPROACH TO THE TEACHING-LEARNING PROCESS

In the process of examining general aspects of the nature of the teaching-learning process, we have uncovered several problem areas, both general and specific. The nature of learning, its measurement, and the question of criteria are not simple matters. There is room for dispute based on both facts and values. Discussion is always in terms of changes in behavior, changes in attitudes, and other observables because there is a profound absence of information about a central facet of the learning mechanism. What happens inside the brain of a person when he learns? No one really knows. If you are shown a new form and are told it is a "Zil," you may well learn this name and use it correctly at some later time.

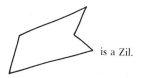 is a Zil.

Something has been learned. Some change has taken place in your brain. This connection has been encoded in such a manner that the correct response can be aroused when the configuration must be identified at some future time. But, to date, science has not identified the nature of the change in the nervous system, nor has it been able to pinpoint its locus. It is not known whether the connection between the visual stimulus and the verbal response exists as a change in the chemistry within some brain cell, or in the physical configuration of a particular cell membrane, or in some aspect of neural transmission. The alternatives just mentioned are only a sample of the many speculations which have been advanced.

If the physical nature of learning were known (and it is part of the faith of the scientist that it will be someday) the problem that has been raised would vanish—that is, assuming there existed a commensurate technology to measure these organic events. Instead of studying performance, an impure manifestation of learning, we would be able to state "Within this brain a relation has been established between A and B." Or, in other terms, the individual has learned to connect A and B and will do so under the constraints of motivation, personality, conflicting responses, and other considerations. This would identify the capacity to perform with the learned connection. Whether the performance would occur is, as we have seen, another matter.

Since, for most practical purposes, the mind of man remains a "black box," it is necessary to deal with the problems of education and learning in terms of the available data that can be observed and related. Even though we do not know the details of what occurs in his brain, it is apparent that a child can learn to read. Also, it can be seen that children learn faster and with fewer undesirable side effects when one teaching technique is used rather than another. One teacher seems to be a "good" teacher, while another is less successful. It is, then, possible to study the empirical relation between input and output. Correlations between certain procedures and probable results can be established. This does not demand a full understanding, however desirable, of the exact mechanisms through which cause and effect operate. The caveman learned to take cover when dark clouds formed, without knowing whether they were a warning from the gods or part of a sequence of natural physical events. And children will continue to learn, as they always have, without waiting for science to complete its analysis. Whatever problems may arise from efforts at definition, people do in fact learn, and they can learn as the result of another's efforts—called teaching.[3]

It is too easy, when considering a social process, to forget about people and leap from abstraction to construct as though discussing the solar system or molecular motion. In education, the concern is with people, and because of this concern, values become part of the corpus of the discipline. Consider the difference between a principle of traditional psychology that might begin, "When an organism is trained to. . . ," and a principle of education that would begin, "When a child is taught to. . . ." It is obvious that in the latter principle, however it is completed, values will emerge that will identify it as a principle of education, regardless of its possible heritage in another discipline.

Essentially, then, our task is to consider a unique relationship between certain significant people—namely, teachers and their students. Since people, both teachers and students, vary widely in personality, ability, and other ways, the relationship is characterized by its purpose rather than its form of expression. What works well for one teacher may not be the best for another, and Bill may be taught by techniques that would not influence Tom at all or would even produce a negative effect. This variability need not mean chaos. It need not mean that it is impossible to formulate principles. A carpenter learns to treat oak differently from pine, and the distinction becomes part of his scheme for working with wood. He may use the same saw but modify his stroke, just as the teacher may use praise of one kind for one student and praise of another kind for a student with a different personality.

PARTICIPANTS IN THE TEACHING-LEARNING PROCESS

DIRECT AND INDIRECT PARTICIPANTS

While the teaching-learning process is usually considered to take the form of direct interaction between a teacher and a learner, there may be mediation over time and distance. A teacher standing in the front of a classroom may teach students a fact or a principle by orally presenting particular material, or the same students may learn the same facts or principles by reading what Plato said long ago. In each case there is a learner, and the material to be learned is the same; but there is a difference in the form of the teaching-learning process. In the classroom presentation the teacher presents the information directly to the students, and together they would seem to completely embody the process. But is this always so? The teacher may well have read Plato and be passing on his concepts to the students. It would seem artificial to exclude Plato from the teaching-learning process when he is read by the teacher and not exclude Plato when he is read by the student. When a man writes a book, his intention is often to teach, and it seems logical to hold that he is still teaching even though there may be one or many intermediaries. Plato, the contemporary teacher, and the students are all involved in the teaching-learning process. The book is a tool, a medium which is used by the teacher to facilitate the process. The teacher may read Plato to the class, recall his teachings from memory, or direct the students to read for themselves. These are a few of the forms the teaching-learning process may take.

Sometimes the teaching-learning process is enriched by other factors. The teacher may be engaged in original research and present his findings directly to the class. New knowledge has been introduced into the culture, and if some of the students become teachers, the cycle will continue. In modern times the teacher-scholar does not depend completely upon his students to carry the word. He usually publishes his work and thus makes it available to other teachers and students removed from him over time and distance. Textbook writers and publishers enter into the teaching-learning process when they take the research efforts of scientists and scholars, organize it, and make the material available to teachers and students. The textbook facilitates the learning of students and the task of the teacher to an inestimable extent.

Others that directly and indirectly affect the teaching-learning process are the administrators of the schools, the educators who train teachers, and those federal, state, and private agencies which grant funds for research in education and the development of new teaching techniques. The influence of these people and agencies becomes obvious when we consider that they are in a position to support some ideas and projects and to withhold endorsement of others. Today, research in education, or any of the other social sciences, is often quite expensive. In order to obtain financial support, a scientist usually submits his research proposal to a fund-granting agency, and if he fails to receive their support, the research may never be completed.

The education enterprise is enormous, and we could mention many kinds of people who become involved to some extent. Next, we will want to consider the unique role of the parents of the young learner.

THE LEARNER AND HIS PARENTS

So far, consideration of the significant people in the teaching-learning enterprise has been devoted to those who are part of the formal structure. It would be a gross oversight to ignore or discount the role of the parent, who is, in a sense, the constant in the educational process. No one would deny the significance of the parent in the development of a child's behavior and attitudes. Yet, many people seem to believe that when the child enters school, the school takes over many of the functions of the parent, and in the area of education especially the parent only needs to ensure that the child arrive at school on time. Many parents would protest that they play a far more important role than this, pointing out that they "make" their children do their homework in the evening. Actually the parent's relation to the teaching-learning process is far more important than that of gatekeeper in the morning and warden in the evening. The failure of many parents to recognize or accept greater responsibility has often complicated the task of the schools and not infrequently has completely thwarted the teacher's efforts. The parents' responsibility is primarily in the area of attitude formation and modification rather than with content learning. As a natural consequence of the process of identification, the child acquires not only the quality but the strength of the attitudes of significant adults around him. Thoughtful parents realize their early influence upon the child's moral character, his speech, his prejudices, even his tastes in food and dress. The small boy wants a hat "just like Daddy wears," and the little girl desires an iron to use while mother is ironing. But despite this insight, many parents do not seem to realize that they have a powerful influence upon their child's attitudes toward both education in general and specific aspects of schooling in particular; or if they are aware, their actions do not reveal it.

The problem is far more complex than simply the development of positive or negative attitudes about such things as eating spinach. However, in some homes, usually at the lowest socioeconomic level, the problem may be just that basic. In homes where the child hears education described as a "waste of time," where teachers are regarded as busybodies, and where the adults constantly talk about the unpleasant aspects of their limited school experience, the child acquires attitudes that will give him an almost insurmountable handicap in school. Usually, attitudes cannot be forced into a good-bad evaluative scale by examining the intrinsic form of the attitude; but instead, it is necessary to examine the effect of the attitude in a particular system. A particular attitude may be an asset in one situation and a liability in another. Attitudes of pacifism may be indispensable to an individual living in a particular community, and yet these same attitudes could be fatal on the battlefield. Attitudes that appear neither good nor bad in their own right could, for the child in school, facilitate or interfere with the teaching-learning process.

It is not only in homes of a low socioeconomic level that children suffer from the formation of the wrong attitudes. Children from homes where education is highly valued and the parents are intensely interested in the schools sometimes suffer when good intentions backfire. Intense pressure for achievement can often produce unfortunate consequences. Sometimes a child will develop a need to achieve and excel that outstrips his capacity to realize goals that have been forced upon him by adults. The parent's conscious motivation may be altruistic but all too often the true motivation is actually selfish. The parent may wish to excel through his child; that is, he may seek vicarious accomplishment of goals that he failed to reach.

Children identify with their parents, but parents also identify with their children. This can be seen when a child passes through a stage of development that was traumatic for the parent as a child, whether some aspect of schooling, social development, or puberty. The parent *relives* his problems, and old tensions, fears, and memories return as he witnesses problems he thought he had solved and forgotten. These problems often are not solved but merely repressed and defended against until they dramatically confront him again through his child. The anxieties of the parent will not pass unnoticed by the child, and the child's problem will be multiplied. If the parent's defenses are too strong, he will be unable to talk with the child or will deny that something is wrong, and the child will not receive emotional support at the time he needs it most. Usually this impasse can be seen most dramatically when it is time for a child to receive sex education. While the parent continues defensive procrastination, the child learns outside the home.

That parents identify with their children can also be seen in the way achievement becomes part of "keeping up with the Joneses." Parents boast of how well their child is reading and even become so specific as to mention how far he has gone in his reader and which reading group he is in. Other parents whose children are the same age feel irritated and even embarrassed if their children have not reached this level of achievement. Without even becoming aware of what they are doing, they begin to put pressure on their children, who shortly come to realize that being in the top reading group is very important. After all, if it were not so important, why would Mother and Father be so concerned?

Another, more subtle, consequence of pressure for achievement is the attitude which develops toward grades. Grades are the measure of achievement which the child sees the parent respond to with approval or disapproval. Too often the child hears that his grades are "not good" or, even more defeatingly, that "the grades are all right, but I know that you can do better." This attitude, fostered in the home, quickly establishes an artificial, extrinsic motive for school performance. These same parents are very shocked if their child is accused of cheating on a test and cannot imagine why he would do such a thing.

Even when the child has the capacity for a high level of achievement, pressure at home for academic mastery can produce unexpected negative attitudes. Often children are bored by classroom activities that are a simple repetition of what they have been taught at home. If the well-meaning parent takes the bright child too far beyond his class in reading or arithmetic, the long-range result may be that the child will find school unchallenging. If the classes are small, permitting special work assignments, or if the school is ungraded, the dangers are lessened, but the risk is not avoided.

It is probably unreasonable to expect parents to avoid teaching their children; the rewards from instructing one's own children, being a part of the teaching-learning process, are too great. Since the parent will want to teach the child, perhaps he should direct his efforts toward enrichment rather than advancement, especially during the early years of school. The parent might then devote his efforts to teaching the child many of the aspects of our culture which are not taught in the schools. Then the activities of the classroom would continue to be new and interesting, and positive attitudes toward formal schooling would continue to grow.

Attitudes can also complicate the task of the schools when the child views the process of education as conflicting with his sex-role identification. This problem is especially acute for the young boy. At the very time in his life when he has formed a strong identification with the father and is learning the masculine role, he is confronted with a social process that may appear quite feminine. Too often, all of his teachers are women, the girls in his class are doing the best work, and his mother helps him with his homework. At the lowest socioeconomic levels of our society this problem is especially prevalent, as here the father is often not a part of the nuclear family.

There seems to be a biological basis for the young girl to be ahead of the boy of the same age in development. (It is known that girl babies learn to walk and learn to talk before boys.) However, the small boy is not in a position to make allowances for this. The early differences between boys and girls are sufficiently pronounced that some educators have even suggested starting boys to school when they are half a year to a year older than the age at which girls start. In addition, it has been shown that teachers are susceptible to unconscious biases and sometimes give girls higher marks than they deserve and boys lower marks. This tendency is independent of whether the teacher is a man or a woman.

It would be very desirable to have more men in the elementary schools, but there are other solutions to the dilemma of the small boy which are the responsibility of the parents, particularly the father. The father must communicate to his son, with both words and actions, that he endorses and approves of education as an institution. This is not difficult. It merely requires taking an active interest in what the child is doing in school and in his homework. Mother can hear the spelling list or the reading as well as father, but to the small boy the involvement of the father changes the whole quality of the activity. To see who carries the burden of concern with the process of early schooling, one has only to look at the large number of mothers relative to the number of fathers in attendance at P.T.A. meetings. The true source of anti-intellectualism may well be in the home rather than in the practices of the schools. These attitudes are not confined to any one social class; even students who intend to go to college minimize their academic interest and efforts. School achievement has been shown to play a very minor role in the adolescent status system, and academic effort often results in negative evaluations from the student's peer group.

Basically, the question is not "should parents teach attitudes toward education?" They cannot avoid this influence on children through either action or inaction any more than can the teacher. Attitudes are usually taught and learned without any intention on the part of teachers or learners. For parents merely to be aware of their influence would in itself be a major step toward rectifying some of the unfortunate practices that exist. Accepting for the moment the thesis that one cannot be with children a significant portion of the day without shaping their attitudes, it follows that it is worth while to give some consideration to the influence they are receiving relevant to education.

The parent is a significant figure in the teaching-learning process in many important ways besides forming and modifying the attitudes of the child. The parent can, and should, serve as the buffer against excessive stress and be the constant, reliable individual in whom the child can confide all troubles, whether they originate in the school or in some other aspect of his life. Whether or not the child has this asset depends on the relation the child and his parents have developed over the years. It is very easy for child and parent to drift apart, to become literally estranged over the years, so slowly that it is almost imperceptible to both.

Even when parents do not press their child to achieve, the child cannot fail to be exposed to the tension which now surrounds education and its relation to the future. Television as well as the less forceful instruments of mass media serve as constant reminders that it is difficult to be admitted to college, that the colleges are overcrowded, and that one should work very hard in school if he wishes to avoid being a failure at eighteen. The wise parent will help the student to handle these stresses and to place them in a reasonable perspective instead of fanning the fires of panic. The confusion of starting at a new school, interaction with new teachers and friends, and adapting to a curriculum with greater demands represent only a few of the adjustments where the considerate parent can be the difference between disaster and smooth transition. Also, the perceptive parent knows his own limitations and seeks outside aid where necessary.

Perhaps one of the most important skills acquired by a learner is study habits. The development of efficient study techniques is often unrelated to general intelligence, and individuals of superior capacity are sometimes handicapped by their lack of study skills. The parent is in a strong position to influence the study habits which the young learner develops. Many of the ways in which the parent can assist the child are a matter of common sense. The parent can provide a place for study that is both quiet and free from distractions. He can try to make sure that study does not begin so late in the evening that fatigue causes the homework to be associated with frustration and lack of interest. The consequences of the parent encouraging the student to "finish your homework and get it over with" are less obvious. When the reward is too strongly attached to the act of completion, quality may be sacrificed for speed. The student who is rushing to complete his home assignment in order to go out and play or watch a favorite television program is similar to the factory employee who is on piece work; that is, he is more concerned with turning out a unit than improving it. Another result is that the student believes that he has completed his task when he reaches the last page of the assigned chapter. Actually the homework is the learning of certain concepts presented in the text, but the true goal is forgotten once the student develops the attitude that "finishing homework" means reading to a certain page. Habits of this variety, once developed, can follow the student through college.

One function of formal education is to transmit the culture from generation to generation. It is from this shared concern of society that a discipline of education is emerging which is based on an attempt to organize the existing knowledge about the teaching-learning process. In this text we shall attempt to examine what is known about learning and teaching. The principles will be principles of education because they will be shaped by a unique concern. The debt to psychology, sociology, and other disciplines will be obvious. There will, however, be no infringement of any discipline's copyrights, for the modifications are significant and the values are a world apart.

THE STUDY OF THE TEACHING-LEARNING PROCESS

The preceding discussion has introduced the protagonists and the supporting cast in the drama of education. Details of the interaction between the significant characters were given to illustrate the complexity of the problem but were by no means intended to be exhaustive. Certain aspects of the interaction between learner, teacher, and parents were pursued in depth to stress the interdependence of these individuals, but other examples would have served as well. The most general problems in the concept of learning were touched upon, and the concept of teaching was given an equally brief treatment. Now the stage is set for a more detailed consideration of the significant people and the real problems encountered in the study of the teaching-learning process.

In the following chapters we will examine what is known about learning as a process and the implications for the effective promotion of learning in the classroom. A consideration of the nature of teaching will reveal its interrelation with both the characteristics of learning and the characteristics of people; for while it may prove possible to approach the general process of learning in an abstract manner as part of the search for scientific principles, its application in the classroom requires significant modification. Each teacher and each student is to some extent a special case. Laws of learning produce normative guides, but they do not constitute inflexible rules. For this reason it will be crucial to consider the teacher and the learner as individuals, not as constants in a learning formula. Laws of learning may contribute to principles of education, but they will never become synonymous with them. The nature of the concern is different, and as a result, the values are different.

•

CHAPTER ONE

Learning:

Theoretical Considerations

•

Men have always, or at least as far back as there are records, wondered about their capacity to learn, to think, and to respond to the world about them. They did not know what internal changes occurred when they thought or learned, but that did not prevent them from conjecture any more than the same lack of information inhibits the theorist of today. Historically, theories of learning, thinking, and behavior were not clearly separate, and indeed, the view that they should not be discrete is quite tenable. To understand the development and meaning of contemporary theories, it is profitable to review the evolution of systems that seek to explain how one element, or one idea, becomes associated with another.

CONNECTIONIST LEARNING THEORIES

CLASSICAL ASSOCIATIONISM

It is customary, and usually safe, to begin with Aristotle (384-322 B.C.) when developing the history of an idea. Learning theory and even associationism as a formal concept were not discussed by

Aristotle, but his speculations about the nature of memory included consideration of the role of *similarity*, *contrast*, and *contiguity* of ideas. These identical dimensions later became prominent in the classical laws of association. Doubtless many other early philosophers should be given credit for their intellectual contributions to the history of association theory, which resulted from their concern with the nature of man and his relation to the universe. For the present, it must be sufficient to acknowledge that the concepts of the mind developed by these early philosophers had, and will continue to have, a profound influence on contemporary theory.

The English school of associationism began with Thomas Hobbes (1588-1679). Hobbes' goal was to give prime importance to the data of the senses as the source of the content of the mind; this approach was in direct opposition to the "innate ideas" of Descartes—the belief that people are born with some kinds of knowledge already a part of their mind. However, the structure of Hobbes' theory was uncertain, and his contribution to associationism was limited. The important figure in this period was John Locke (1632-1704), and he should be regarded as the real leader, little influenced by Hobbes. For Locke, too, the emphasis was on the role of experience and of sensation which make their record on the *tabula rasa*, the blank slate of the mind. This formulation may be seen as the origin of English empiricism with its emphasis upon the role of the environment which characterizes the intellectual heirs of classical associationism today. The term *associationism* was not used extensively by Locke, who spoke mainly of "connections," or combinations of ideas. The theory of associationism owes its name to Locke's "Of the Association of Ideas," a critical chapter in his *Essay on Human Understanding* (1690).

David Hume (1711-1776) made significant contributions to the theory of association, though he too did not press the use of the term. For Hume, associations occurred as the result of a force or attraction that caused the ideas to come together and unite. He also was led to the proposition that these attractions of ideas are in fact *tendencies* since they do not always occur. The influence of this notion is seen today in the fact that association data are treated statistically rather than by analyses based on all-or-nothing models. As a result of empirical study, it becomes possible to state the probability that a particular association will occur in a given population or for a particular individual. There is, however, no guarantee that a certain association will occur every time. The notion that associations may result from elements that are linked through other elements was Hume's anticipation of what is now referred to as *mediated association*. For example, the word *red* might cause me to think of *barn*, which in turn leads to the association *cow*. In this instance *red* led to *cow* through the mediation of the concept *barn*. Such chains may be quite long and complex, branching in many directions, and they contribute to the richness and diversity of human thought.

It was David Hartley (1707-1757) who made associationism a doctrine. His laws for the body and the mind are difficult to separate. Essentially he believed that when a set of sensations becomes associated with another set often enough, the first set obtains a power over the corresponding set so that when sensations of the first set are impressed upon the mind alone, they excite the ideas of the second set. The phrase "often enough" is interesting because it recognizes the fact that functional learning does not necessarily occur as the result of a sole occurrence of two elements in a particular relationship. This does not mean, however, that the learning mechanism is inefficient; for if every chance relationship were to be permanently recorded, our store of meaningless relationships would be endless. If learning is maximal when relationships are repeated some number of times, there is an optimal solution to the problem of learning the valid relationships that exist in the environment. It seems reasonable that the learning mechanism would not have evolved past the functionally significant level it has now obtained because a higher level would not give an increase in selective advantage. (Bright people are not more likely to have children than those of average intelligence.)

The notion that association was mental compounding, the simple addition of elements, was stressed by James Mill (1773-1836). "Thought follows thought, idea follows idea, incessantly." For James Mill, association was a matter of contiguity (concurrence) and involved no forces or attractions. His belief that associations vary in strength became important in later theories. For some modern theorists, the strength of an association refers to its likelihood of occurrence. Strength, then, refers to a statistical attribute of the association.

The contribution of the more famous Mill, John Stuart Mill (1806-1873), was to substitute mental chemistry for mental mechanics. "The associative whole is more than a sum of parts." He stated four principles of association—similarity, frequency, contiguity, and inseparability. Alexander Bain (1818-1903) should be mentioned here for contributing the notion of compound association. His view was that associations can operate together and arouse past learning that the individual associations could not. For example, *beauty* and *ships* may lead to the association *Helen* when either stimulus alone would not have had that effect. The analogy to chemistry is that water has attributes which cannot be predicted from the knowledge of the attributes of hydrogen and oxygen.

Not all associationists took the position that one idea becomes attached to another in fixed pattern or permanent structure. For Johann Friedrich Herbart (1776-1841), association was a dynamic process. There is a totality of conscious ideas, an *apperceptive mass* into which new ideas are assimilated. The mass is constantly changing, and its momentary state determines the encoding of new material. Ideas constantly interact, they have energy of their own, and the dynamic interplay never ceases.

Related to the apperceptive mass is the concept of the schema. For H. Head, the schema consists of organized past impressions; a person has a "model" of himself which constantly changes. The schema refers to physiological dispositions. As H. Head defined it, "For this combined standard against which all subsequent changes of posture are measured before they enter consciousness, we propose the word 'schema.'"[1] And F. C. Bartlett stated:

> "Schema" refers to an active organization of past re-actions, or of past experiences, which must always be supposed to be operating in any well-adapted organic response.[2]
>
> What, precisely does the 'schema' do? Together with the preceding incoming impulse it renders a specific adaptive reaction possible. It is, therefore, producing an orientation of the organism towards whatever it is directed to at the moment. But that orientation must be dominated by the immediately preceding reaction or experiences. To break away from this the 'schema' must become not merely something that works the organism, but something with which the organism can work. . . . So the organism discovers how to turn round on its own 'schemata,' or in other words, it becomes conscious.[3]
>
> The influence of 'schemata' is influence by the past. But the differences are at first sight profound. In its schematic form the past operates en masse, or, strictly, not quite en masse, because the latest incoming constituents which go to build up a 'schema' have a predominant influence.[4]

CONNECTIONISM

Modern psychologists who owe a debt to classical associationism are often called connectionists or S-R (stimulus-response) theorists. Instead of being concerned with how ideas become related, they place more emphasis on the manner in which a particular response becomes connected to, or associated with, a specific stimulus or situation. This school begins with Edward L. Thorndike at the end of the nineteenth century. Thorndike, a student of

William James, took the big step of abandoning consideration of the chain of ideas within the organism and concentrating on the relation between behavior and the environmental surroundings.

Thorndike's early studies of baby chickens serves well to illustrate the distinction between his approach and that of the classical associationists. Thorndike was unhappy about a model that described a chick pecking food in terms of a series of ideas in the mind of the chick. He did not deny that such "ideas" may exist in the chick, but he felt that it was much safer to simply describe the fact that the sight of food was *connected* to the response of pecking. Thorndike was not anti-introspection, as many psychologists have been, but rather reserved introspection for the study and explanation of human behavior. He was not the last psychologist to wield Occam's razor of parsimony in the formulation of a behavior theory. While there are commanding arguments for simplicity as a criterion for choosing between alternative theories, it must always be remembered that there is no guarantee that the parsimonious explanation is the correct one. Nature does not always conform to the topology of the mind of man.

The central principle of learning advanced by Thorndike was the *law of effect*. This principle, which was developed at the beginning of the twentieth century as a part of connectionism, states that an act is altered by its consequences. The law of effect is a principle of trial and error as the basis of learning. Thorndike conducted many experiments. At that time experiments were beginning to be widely used by psychologists in an effort to support their theories with empirical data.

The study of animals learning to escape from puzzle boxes provided Thorndike with much of his basic conception of trial-and-error learning. To escape Thorndike's puzzle box, a cat had to pull on a string, a response which had not yet been learned. The situation produced many responses from the animal; most of them did not work, a few did. On future trials the cat would produce fewer and fewer of those responses that did not produce a favorable effect, and those responses that did produce a favorable effect (escape) became more frequent. For Thorndike, the interpretation was that as the result of experience some tendencies (responses) became stronger and others became weaker. The layman views the mastery of some skill in much the same manner. The golfer reports that with practice he is achieving longer drives (more correct responses) and seldom hooks the ball (fewer incorrect responses).

Behaviorism was the extreme form of connectionism fathered by J. B. Watson (beginning circa 1912). Introspection was out, and the entire emphasis was on the description of overt behavior, performance, and the role of the environment. Mental events were not considered a part of scientific psychology. What a person *said* might be valid data but what he *meant* was unknowable.

> Behaviorism thus leaves out speculations. You'll find in it no reference to the intangibles—the unknown and the unknowable 'psychic entities.' The behaviorist has nothing to say of 'consciousness.' How can he? Behaviorism is a natural science. He has neither seen, smelled nor tasted consciousness nor found it taking part in any human reactions.[5]

This school was dominant up until about 1930, but then the pendulum began to swing back. Most psychologists today realize that classical behaviorism precludes study of the richest and most significant facets of human experience. Perhaps it is the psychologist's increasing confidence in the intellectual integrity of his subject matter that has allowed him to adopt some of the methods of the humanities to complement techniques of the traditional sciences.

Before leaving early connectionism, we should note that many of these theorists had very definite ideas about the nature of the connections central to their system. Their theories were strongly influenced by the expanding science of physiology in the nineteenth century, and the connections were often conceived of as neural connections, or changes in the synapses between one neural unit and another. It seemed quite reasonable to suppose that there would be a close correspondence between neural anatomy and behavioral changes. To understand the development of contemporary learning theories, we will now turn to the study of conditioned responses.

CONDITIONED RESPONSE LEARNING

Ivan Pavlov (1849-1936), a Russian physiologist, discovered that under certain circumstances a response would become conditional upon the occurrence of a stimulus which previously did not elicit the response. In a series of classical experiments, he found that meat placed in the mouth of a dog evoked salivation as a reflexive, or unlearned, response. Salivation is called an unconditioned response (UCR) to food which is the unconditioned stimulus (UCS). The term *unconditioned* is used because the relation between the stimulus and the response does not depend upon conditioning (learning). The sound of a bell does not cause a dog to salivate; it is not a stimulus for that response. If the sound of the bell is presented immediately before placing the meat in the dog's mouth, and if this process is repeated many times, the bell sound will acquire the capacity to produce salivation when it is presented alone. The bell sound has become a conditioned stimulus (CS) for salivation which is now a conditioned response (CR) to the bell sound. If a new stimulus, perhaps a light, is paired with the bell sound, the new stimulus may become a CS for salivation. Through this operation of higher order conditioning, stimuli far removed from the original UCS may come to elicit the response.

Pavlov also found that if the bell sound was repeated many times without the food, it would gradually lose its capacity to elicit salivation. The tendency for the bell sound to elicit salivation could be maintained if *reinforced* occasionally by again pairing the bell sound with the food. Both the terms *conditioning*, which is now often used to mean learning in general, and *reinforcement* are used in other theories with different implications. The response conditioned by Pavlov was a reflex. A reflex is a relatively stereotyped innate response to a specific stimulus. For example, the human eye-blink reflex can be conditioned by pairing a signal with a puff of air (UCS) that strikes the eye. After many pairings, the signal alone will elicit the eye-blink reflex.

Most psychologists believe that the conditioning of *respondent* (reflexive) behavior is a quite different process from the learning of voluntary behavior. Voluntary behavior is sometimes called *operant* because the individual appears to be "operating" on the world rather than responding automatically. In the case of operant behavior, like walking and talking, it is not possible to identify the specific stimuli for the responses. Behavior appears to be emitted rather than elicited. It is assumed that voluntary behavior is the result of a stimulus, but the form of the stimulus is often obscure. If a person says "How are you today?" the question is not the direct stimulus for a response. We may reply "Fine" or "Not so good," or we may regard the question as rhetorical and not reply. The original question is the stimulus for a complex series of internal associations that mediate between the external stimulus and the final reply. The reply is voluntary in that the speaker can "choose" among many alternative responses. Many social responses are culturally overdetermined and hence seem automatic, but special circumstances will reveal their voluntary nature.

Some investigators have emphasized the fact that learning is produced by the contiguity of the response with a given situation. E. R. Guthrie, whose theory does not emphasize the role of the reinforcing stimulus, would maintain that the important factor in conditioning salivation to a bell sound is that salivation occurred originally at the same time as the bell sound. True, the food produced the salivation, but all that is required for learning is that the response occur in a given situation, and that situation will then elicit the response in the future. If a small boy slams the screen door, the proper strategy for his desperate parents, according to this theory, is to be sure that he closes the door properly as his last response. That is, whenever the boy slams the door, he should be called back and made to go out again without slamming the door. In this way the desired response, closing the door quietly, is learned because it is made at the same time that the child sees the door or is in the door "situation." A desirable response has been substituted for an undesirable one by guaranteeing that the right response occurs last in the critical situation. The theory does not ignore the obvious fact that rewards and goals facilitate learning but holds that they function only to change the situation—to terminate behavior and, as a result, determine what will be the last response in the situation. According to this formulation, anything that terminated the sequence of behavior at the right time would be equally effective.

COMPLEX CONNECTIONISM

Elements of both reinforcement and substitution can be found in Clark Hull's reinforcement theory. If a drive or a need is reduced, all previous behavior is reinforced. When any response occurs, there are many stimulus elements present in addition to those stimuli which produced the response. When the response produces drive reduction, not only is the relation between the specific stimulus and response strengthened (law of effect), but cross-connections with all other stimuli that happen to be present are also strengthened (substitution). This is an oversimplification, but Hullian theory is quite complex, and it is not possible to do it full justice here.

O. H. Mowrer and others have introduced two-factor theories of learning that, in essence, state that some parts of the total learning process are by simple contiguity and other parts are by need reduction or effect. To illustrate, suppose a child falls from a horse and is badly frightened. By simple contiguity, fear becomes attached to the sight or idea of horses because a horse was the predominant stimulus in the situation that accompanied the fear response. Need reduction functions later when the child is again confronted with a horse. The sight of the horse is now a CS for fear or anxiety, but when the child avoids the animal, the anxiety is reduced. The reduction of anxiety serves to reinforce the avoidance response. The child has, then, developed a phobia toward horses that evolved from two separate processes—fear associated with the horse by contiguity and avoidance learned through need reduction.

While not connectionist in the traditional sense, the analysis used by B. F. Skinner should be mentioned at this time. His emphasis is upon the emitted response, the operant behavior of the organism. If a small child is placed in a room where there is a specially constructed candy machine with a lever, the child will walk around, touch objects in the room, and explore in general. All of this behavior is operant. Eventually the child will touch the lever, and if he moves it correctly, a piece of candy will appear. It will not be long before he pulls the lever again and again. He has learned to make a particular response. But let us examine what has happened. The first time the lever was pulled, there had been no previous reinforcement. The response was not elicited automatically as a reflex. If nothing happened the first time the child touched the lever, he would still touch it again occasionally if left in the room. The rate at which the response occurs naturally is called the *operant level* of the response. Under different drive conditions the operant level of a given response will vary. A hungry organism will emit many diverse responses, each at a greater rate than when it is not hungry. Learning is shown by the change in the rate at which the response occurs under constant or unvarying drive conditions.[6]

Any stimulus that increases the rate at which a response occurs is called a *positive reinforcer* of the response. The candy is a positive reinforcer because it increases the rate of the response. If the child received electric shocks when he touched the lever, the rate of the response would fall below the operant level. The electric shock would be punishment for the response of touching the lever. Popularly speaking, candy is a reward, and electric shock is a punishment. What makes this analysis different from traditional connectionism is that the emphasis is on the changing probability of a response, not on the changing of the bond between a situation and a response.

The term *negative reinforcement* refers to a different operation than does punishment. Negative reinforcement is noxious stimulation which is given because the organism is *not* giving some desired response. Electric shocks administered to a rat until he terminates them by pressing a lever would be an example. Often the distinction between punishment and negative reinforcement is a matter of behavior contingencies. When a teacher admonishes a student for being noisy, this is punishment for causing a commotion, but it is at the same time negative reinforcement for behaving correctly. To tell a student that he is wrong when he states that oxygen is the most common gas is punishment of that response according to the definition. However, the term *punishment* has many popular connotations which are misleading. It would give the wrong impression, though it would be technically true, if we were to refer to the teacher as one who punishes wrong responses and positively reinforces correct responses. We shall describe this activity of the teacher as letting the student know when he is wrong and rewarding him when he is right.

The reinforcement of a student's correct responses with "good" is actually an example of *secondary reinforcement.* Stimuli associated with a reinforcing situation acquire the capacity to reinforce behavior by themselves. If a rat is fed when he presses a lever, he learns this performance. A light flash paired with the food will come to be a reinforcer and can be used alone to produce further learning. The small child hears "good" pronounced in situations accompanied by physical affection and other positive treatment, with the result that the verbal symbol becomes adequate for purposes of modifying behavior. To become a secondary reinforcer, a stimulus must be present during primary reinforcement of a correct response and absent when the response and primary reinforcement are absent. Words of praise do not become reinforcers if they are given to a child independently of his behavior. Indiscriminate use of praise obviously causes it to lose its significance. The same is true of admonition, or punishment.

REINFORCEMENT VERSUS CONTIGUITY

To summarize, there are three main positions on the question of the importance of reinforcement. One position holds that for learning to occur there must be motivation or drive present and learning results when that drive is reduced, or when an effect is produced, pleasurable or otherwise (i.e., positive reinforcement or punishment). Hull is representative of this position; though Thorndike is usually included, he did not insist that the law of effect was relevant to all varieties of learning. In opposition to this formulation are those theories that hold contiguity, not effect, to be the important factor in learning. This view is typified by Guthrie. The third group are those who believe that contiguity and effect are two distinct learning processes which operate in different situations. Thorndike, Skinner, and Mowrer belong in this group.

This controversy has produced a great deal of research and discussion in the past, and the evidence presented by one group has often been interpreted in quite a different manner by advocates of another position. For on the one hand it is easy to find situations where reward or reinforcement facilitates learning, while on the other it is possible to show cases where learning occurs without any obvious drive reduction or apparent reinforcement. We have seen how contiguity theory attempts to cope with the obvious efficacy of rewards by holding that they merely terminate the behavior sequence so that the right response is the last response. The reinforcement and drive reduction theorists have their own explanation for the experiments of the contiguity theorists that purport to show learning without drive reduction. One way is to state that some drive is reduced even if it cannot be identified. If a rat shows later that it has learned something about a maze in which it wandered randomly, some theorists would claim that it had learned without any reinforcement required. But those theorists who hold that reinforcement is critical for learning can argue that perhaps the rat has an "exploratory drive" which is reduced as he wanders about and that this is the reinforcement. In many ways the question becomes a pseudo-problem, for it is impossible to prove whether or not some unknown drive exists. Similarly, going back to the example of having the child come back and close the door properly, the reinforcement theorist could argue that this is not simple contiguity because it is punishment to call the child back at all.

Fortunately, the dilemma of the theorists does not alter the fact that children do learn aspects of what they experience. And for that matter, so does the rat, independently of the theoretical position of the experimenter.

NONCONNECTIONIST LEARNING THEORIES

One group of psychologists has been notable in emphasizing the structure people impose upon their experience rather than the roles of effect or contiguity. The *Gestalt* psychologists Max Wertheimer, Kurt Koffka, and Wolfgang Köhler reacted against associationism and stressed the importance of organization. Perception was their commanding concern, but learning also received considerable attention. Learning for these field theorists consists of a reorganization of the world of experience.

To use an example employing Kurt Lewin's topological analysis, suppose a child's beach ball rolls into the water. If he is afraid of the water, the water is a barrier between him and his goal, the ball. Figure I.1 represents the life space of the child. When after a while the child realizes that the only way to his goal is to have his mother help him, he reorganizes his life space. (See Figure I.2) When the ball again goes into the water, he will run again to recruit his mother's aid, instead of tearfully watching the ball float away. He has learned what to do, and for the field theorist this means that there has been a reorganization of the child's psychological world. Since people organize all of their experience, learning becomes a special case of a pervasive tendency, and attention is directed to principles of organization and structure instead of to laws of learning. The emphasis is not on links between stimuli and responses or even situations and responses, but on the entire person functioning in a total environment as it exists psychologically for the individual.

The critics of this approach claim that it is not a theory of behavior but rather a description. They believe that descriptions of the life space and of goals are arrived at by working backwards from observable behavior and that if one is actually studying behavior, that is what should be described, rather than a hypothetical man-world model. The followers of Lewin have countered by claiming that when they discover the principles that govern the way people form structures and organize experience, they can predict how a person will respond. Implicit in the notion is that the past experience of the individual is unimportant if you know everything about him as he is now. But no one would argue that the past acts at a distance. While we are changed as a result of past experience, what we do is determined by what we are right now.

Akin to the field theories and distinct from traditional connectionism is the psychology of E. C. Tolman. For Tolman, learning consists of a person developing a new expectancy or new insight. To use the example of the door-slamming boy again, Tolman might say that the boy learns that closing the door quietly permits him to join his friends at play. He also develops the expectancy that if he slams the door, he will be called back and his plans will be interrupted.

When a rat learns a maze or a child learns to find certain references in the library, they form new cognitions. Which "cognitive map" is employed by an individual depends upon what he wishes to do. One goal will arouse and cause a person to use one cognitive map, while a different goal will cause him to follow other cognitions. The emphasis on what the individual *wants* to do has led some to consider Tolman a *purpovist*. Purpovists hold, in gen-

FIGURE I.1. *Original Life Space of Child*

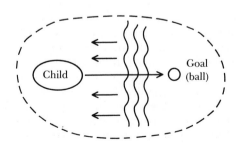

FIGURE I.2. *Reorganized Life Space of Child*

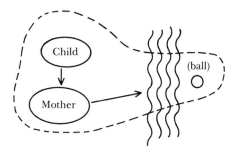

eral, that it is only when we know a person's goals, what he is after, that his behavior becomes meaningful.

In contrast to the S-R (stimulus-response) theorists, Tolman is the central figure in situation-expectation theory. Perception is what is important, and the perceptual nature of learning makes learning compatible with the rest of an individual's experiences. As a result of contiguity, experiences come to create expectations which are aroused later by similar situations. Fundamentally, the concept is directly related to the association of "ideas" which concerned the early associationists.

SUMMARY OF THE PRIMARY DISTINCTIONS BETWEEN LEARNING THEORIES

While all learning theories differ in some or many details, two major distinctions are of interest. One distinction has to do with the nature of learning itself. For some theorists learning is a connection formed between a stimulus and a response (S-R), for some it is the connection between a situation and a response, while for still other theorists learning is a perceptual change, situation-expectation. This is the connectionist versus nonconnectionist controversy.

The other manner in which learning theories may be differentiated is by the conditions which are required in order for learning to occur. This is the reinforcement versus contiguity controversy. There seem to be two major views. One is that there must be some "effect" of an action or some reinforcement, while the opposed position holds that all that is necessary is that the correct response be the last. A third position attempts a rapprochement; there are two distinct learning processes, reinforcement is required for one variety of learning but not for the other.

Differences among learning theories concerning the nature of learning could actually be independent of differences over the necessity for reinforcement, but historically they are not. Theorists who hold that reinforcement is necessary are also usually S-R psychologists, while perceptual change psychologists tend to find reinforcement unimportant in their formulations. The fact that there are exceptions suggests that the correlation between the two issues is not logically required.

OTHER CONTROVERSIES

Thus far we have been considering the major themes in learning theory, but controversies have also existed over many smaller issues. It may be fruitful to examine some of the more famous issues.

PROBLEM SOLVING

In a problem-solving situation a person begins by making various responses, most of which do not work; i.e., wrong responses. The problem is considered solved when the person consistently makes responses that work, i.e., right responses. The learning process by which the person changes from producing wrong responses to producing correct responses does not always appear to be the same. Sometimes we see a gradual elimination of wrong responses. That is, each time the person works on the problem, which is called a *trial*, he makes fewer mistakes. He seems to try first one approach and then another, retaining some approaches and rejecting others. *Trial and error* is the phrase used to describe problem learning that appears to have these characteristics. At other times we see something quite different. The person starts out on the problem and at first does not seem to be making very much progress; then suddenly he makes correct responses and continues to do so. His performance has jumped from a low level of adequacy to complete or near-complete problem solution without any apparent gradual elimination of incorrect responses. The term *insight* has been used to describe this sudden change in performance. (See Figure I.3)

The concept of insight in psychology is essentially the same as its popular connotation. The individual appears to have suddenly *seen* into the problem rather than to have improved gradually. It is interesting that legend has many of the great concepts of science resulting from insight. Most people know the story of Archimedes in his bath who "suddenly" developed the concept of specific gravity when he noticed how his body displaced water. Whether or not Archimedes actually ran through the streets shout-

FIGURE I.3. *The Acquisition of New Behavior by Insight Versus Trial and Error*

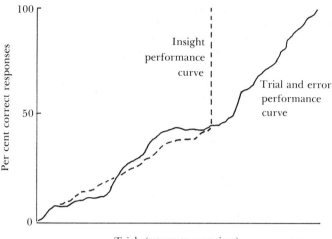

ing "Eureka," insight is often thought of as a sort of Eureka phenomenon. Very similar in concept is the tale of Newton under the apple tree, and other examples from folklore are legion. Perhaps any accounting of insight during idle moments should include the experiences of individuals, such as Lewis Carroll, who claim to have suddenly awakened during the night with a solution to some problem. The particular stories may not be true, but the phenomenon of a sudden improvement in performance cannot be denied.

The important consideration is, however, that we are looking at performance and performance changes, not at the processes that produce performance change. It is possible that a person may "try out" many approaches to a problem by a symbolic process without any noticeable change in his overt behavior. Perhaps the analysis of a hypothetical problem may clarify the issue. Consider the task of learning to find one's way from the outside of a maze or labyrinth to a goal in the center. When a person enters the maze for the first time, he wanders about trying first one path and then another before finally coming upon the goal. After completing this first trial, he starts over again from the outside. If each time he enters a blind alley is considered a mistake, anything he learned on the first trial would result in fewer mistakes on the second trial. He may remember that he should turn right at the first choice point and right again at the second choice point. By trial and error, the wrong turns can be gradually eliminated until he can go through the maze consistently without error.

However, something quite different could occur. Some individuals might begin to wonder if perhaps the maze is not random but has some pattern. After discovering that the first two correct choices are right turns and the second two are left turns, they might form the hypothesis that this is a repeating pattern. If in fact it is, the result would be a sudden change in maze performance from inadequate to perfect. Or they may recall that the fifth and sixth choices do not fit their hypothesis and abandon it for a different hypothesis. This symbolic trial and error would not necessarily be observable, only the sudden change in performance which is the result of insight would be noticeable.

It should be noted that only certain problems will permit "insight." If the maze was random, if there was no principle in its construction, it would have to be learned by rote. Each correct turn would have to be learned by trial and error since there is no principle to discover. Indeed, if there is no principle involved, the formulation of a hypothesis could interfere with mastery. The individual would be formulating hypotheses when he should be concentrating on a rote learning task. An interesting paradox presents itself. The intelligent, creative individual may be under a handicap in some learning situations that would present no problem to those less able. While the creative individual is formulating hypotheses, the less able individual may solve the problem by persisting through trial and error. Once in a while an individual is found to have difficulty mastering some simple task because "he knows too much." Some individuals who have made significant contributions to their culture in the sciences or arts were regarded as impractical people by their friends and associates. Often the accusation was justified, as the rote problems of daily life are most efficiently handled by those who do not search constantly for some higher abstraction or meaning. It is a rare man who can engage in constructive fantasy one moment and switch to the practical treatment of mundane problems the next.

Returning to the insights of great scientists and other famous thinkers, it can usually be shown that they had spent a great amount of time considering the particular problem and had at their intellectual disposal all the elements of the solution. It is impossible to estimate the extent to which their sudden revelations were based on a mountain of implicit trial and error. What is important is that they solved the problems, and if we were to discard the concept of "insight" to explain the process, it would not in any way detract from their accomplishments.

The concept of trial and error would obviously have appeal for association theorists. The "effect" of one trial versus another in producing a total pattern makes the information compatible with the views of reinforcement. There is also a basic compatibility between the concept of perceptual change and the concept of insight. However, care must be taken not to beg the question of what produces the perceptual reorganization. The question is not a simple one, and research on it will continue for a long time to come.

Another interesting problem, and one of paramount importance to education, is the question of learning as a skill. Is learning a skill in the sense that it can be learned or improved? We can answer yes if we are careful how we view the important variables. People can learn to produce changes in their performance. If an individual is given the task of memorizing literary selections, it can be shown that as a result of experience he is able to master comparable selections in shorter and shorter lengths of time. This can be seen only if there are certain restrictions. The time between tasks cannot be so short as to produce fatigue or interference from the material itself.

There is no evidence that the innate capacity to learn changes; rather, it seems that a person can learn to make better use of his capacity. He can learn ways of eliminating distraction and interference, and he can learn superior techniques of organizing his approach to the task. Also, he may learn something about concentration and directing his attention to the relevant aspects of the material.

There are many different strategies that people use to increase their learning efficiency. One is the mnemonic aid. Some things that an individual has to learn are not related by any principle or framework. For example, to learn the connection between the name Columbus and the date 1492 is a rote learning task. The relation is a fact in isolation; it cannot be learned with the aid of a meaningful intellectual superstructure. But the use of the mnemonic "In 1492 Columbus sailed the ocean blue" makes the date easier to remember. Similar is the device for learning people's names by associating the name with some characteristic, "Mr. Brice seems very nice." Other associations can intrude, with the result that Mr. Brice is called Mr. Good or Mr. Nice, but in general the technique does work. If a person using this technique learns the names of other people faster than he did before, is it correct to conclude that he has learned to learn? Yes, if care is taken to remember exactly what is meant by the statement. There are many other strategies one can learn to facilitate learning, and many of these constitute what is meant by good study habits. Included would be assuring freedom from distraction, studying first the whole and then the parts (if the material has a total organization), self-testing, and review.

At this point the *set to learn*—or, less formally, a predisposition to learn—should be mentioned.[7] When reading a novel for pleasure, one quite commonly finds when he has finished that he has no recall for the names of many of the characters or places mentioned in the plot. Yet if one knew that he would be tested on what he had read, he could read it with a different attitude and retain this information. It would appear that in some situations the desire to learn results in learning. Attitudes seem to be very important in learning, and it may well be that one aspect of learning to learn consists in bringing certain attitudes to bear when dealing with a learning task.

IMPRINTING

A controversial form of learning which may have implications for education is imprinting. It is well known that many organisms possess an instinctual capacity for quite complex behavior. Instinctive behavior mechanisms are inherited and do not require learning. The spider constructs an elaborate web based on a design that is characteristic of the individual species. Another species erects a web that is quite different but equally complex. The web-building occurs without learning, and a spider isolated since it first emerged from the egg still produces a perfect web when mature. Natural history provides us with many similar examples. One point is important: for behavior to be instinctive, it does not necessarily have to be apparent from birth. While the potential is always present, the complex instinctual pattern may not be released until a particular stage of maturation is reached or until the organism is in an adequate situation. The nest-building behavior of birds is another case in point.

Imprinting has components similar to instincts, but it involves learning.[8] The classic example of imprinting is a phenomenon observed with newly hatched ducks. The ducklings will follow any moving object in their environment. This predisposition reaches peak strength about sixteen hours after they have hatched. Whatever object they happen to follow during this period, they also *learn* to follow. That is, in the future they will follow the object they imprinted upon during the critical period and will not follow other moving objects if given a choice. Normally ducklings imprint upon the mother duck; but if a man is present alone during the critical period, they will imprint upon him and will follow the man rather than an adult duck in the future. There is, then, an innate predisposition for a particular variety of learning to take place.

Similarly, it has been found that if puppies are isolated from people for their first six months of life, they will never develop the normal affectional behavior toward people characteristic of the house pet. One explanation seems to be that this learning must happen early or not at all; the dogs must imprint upon people during an early critical period, and if this does not occur, the results cannot be undone.

Unproven, but not impossible, is that the social learning of humans may be under the control of a similar mechanism. Perhaps the early social learning and attitudes developed by children are not replaceable by later learning. That is to say, a child who fails to imprint upon others at some critical stage may never again be able to learn some social attitudes or form certain relationships with others. In support of the importance of the early years is the known difficulty of changing the sociopathic individual through therapy. The problem of the teacher who must work with children who lack certain social values and needs is obvious. For the moment, it should be noted that some social deficiencies may possibly represent a lack of social learning that is very difficult to correct because the critical period is past.

There may be other examples of imprinting in humans. One possibility is in the area of speech development, which also appears to have a critical learning period. The individual who does not learn to speak early in life because of a defect of hearing seems to be at an extreme disadvantage in learning to speak later after the defect is corrected.

THEORETICAL CONTROVERSY AND CLASSROOM PRACTICE

The reaction of the educator to these disparate theories and special questions of learning might well be, "Yes, but what should I do in order to teach successfully? What help do these theories offer me in choosing one teaching procedure over another?" Basically, it seems that the fact that there are various theories of learning does not imply that dramatically different classroom procedures should be used. One set of theories may call for adequate reinforcement, but other theories would endorse the same procedure on the basis of a different formulation. If one theory led to teaching procedures clearly different from those suggested by another theory, the relative efficacy of the two approaches could be determined.

There are commanding reasons why the choice of teaching procedures should never be based directly upon theories of learning. First, theories of learning attempt to explain why learning has taken place; disputes over whether or not learning has occurred in a given case are rare. If a teaching technique produces results, most learning theories would be able to explain why learning occurred in terms of their own system though one theory would emphasize one aspect of the process more than another aspect.

Two observations can be made concerning theory and practice. The first is that at times specific techniques and methods based on a specific theoretical orientation have been introduced into the classroom, but their ultimate retention is based not on the acceptance of any theory but on the fact that they work. Any method that did not produce the desired results would not be retained regardless of the theory behind it. A second consideration is that theories of learning are not modified by values, while principles of education are the result of both empirical learning facts and a special value system. The empirical determinants of learning can be studied and those, together with a philosophy of education that contains a value system, will determine classroom practice.

•

CHAPTER TWO

Structuring a Discipline

of

Education

•

The empirical knowledge that is available about learning has resulted from two principal sources of inquiry. One source has been the research inspired by learning theories such as those discussed in the preceding chapter. A cardinal property of any good theory is that it is stated in a form that permits testing. Whether true or false, a theory that provides an incentive for research by suggesting testable hypotheses will result in an addition to knowledge. The second source of inquiry is the concern of educators who search for better means of bringing about learning in the classroom. The educator may discover that learning is facilitated more by one technique than by another. Possibly neither technique is the result of a theory but has emerged in practice because it produced some desired result. If one teaching technique produces more learning than another, it seems obvious that something has been discovered about both the nature of learning and the science of teaching, and it is a sterile distinction to say that effective classroom procedures are more related to teaching than learning.

CLASSROOM HYPOTHESES

Specific hypotheses will be inspired by observation in the classroom. The educator motivated by his concern with teaching will observe the way students behave in the school environment. This experience can result in the formation of specific hypotheses. For example, observation of children in a particular school may reveal that they do not respond to approval or other social rewards offered by the teacher, but that they are responsive to these same rewards from their peer group. This informal study may lead to the specific, testable hypothesis that a teaching technique that utilizes peer-group rewards may produce more learning than the technique currently in use.

Also, research in methods of teaching can be directed at different levels of appraisal. We can ask the pragmatic question, "Which method is better for accomplishing our purpose—the use of teaching machines or the use of some traditional teaching technique?" This question is a practical one, similar to conducting tests to determine which fabric will give the longest service in a suit. Another level of appraisal would be to study the attributes of different methods. Do students learn more when they work in a group, or when they work individually? Is highly organized material easier to learn than material interspersed with nonessential information? Does immediate feedback result in more effective learning than delayed knowledge of performance? These questions are at the same level as asking what makes some fabrics last longer than others. Is it the type of fiber? Fiber length? Is it the weave?

Analyses of this kind open the way for interesting innovations. It could well be that the best aspects of several methods could be used together, resulting in a technique superior to the existing ones. Hypothetically, suppose that teaching machines were shown to be superior to most lectures because of the greater organization of the material. We might discover that if this degree of organization were brought into the lecture, the lecture method would surpass the machine. Other examples can readily be imagined, but the point is that when considering specific factors we are engaged in the scientific study of the teaching-learning process much more so than when we compare complex teaching techniques where it is impossible to determine *why* one technique produces better results than the other.

PROBLEMS WITH EMPIRICAL RESEARCH

In considering what is known about learning from empirical investigations, there are certain pitfalls that the educator should avoid. Caution is required because the educator is not primarily concerned with learning in general but specifically with learning in the classroom. And this concern requires important qualifications.

One immediate problem is that a great many principles of learning are the result of laboratory studies of animal behavior under highly controlled conditions. For the conclusions of these experiments to have implications for the teacher, it must be shown that humans behave in some analogous manner in the classroom. Even when the subjects of learning experiments are people, variables that are critical in the laboratory may be unimportant in the classroom and factors may be present in the classroom that are ignored in the laboratory study. Research in the classroom is the only satisfactory method for evaluating the implications of laboratory results for education. Even then, experienced investigators know that caution is required. What works for one tenth-grade class may not be useful for other grades or even for other tenth-grades. Additional research is required to determine if an educational technique developed with one population of students is also effective with different populations. There are other problems; for example, a technique may produce results only because it is new. Lengthy investigation is required to discover whether or not a promising technique appears good because of a *novelty effect* which will soon wear off with the result that there has been little gain.

After these objections have been met, it may be found that the application of a particular principle would violate some of the values of education. A principle of learning may suggest a teaching technique which proves to be a very effective way to produce learning; but if it is in opposition to certain values, it will be rejected by the educator. The values might be humanitarian, or they might have to do with the goals of the school. For example, techniques which produce undesirable attitudes as side effects will not be adopted. Inducing children to learn for a specific reward might cause them to learn more but at the same time prevent them from discovering the intrinsic values of knowledge.

THE DEVELOPMENT OF EDUCATIONAL PRINCIPLES

Table II.1 illustrates how facts about the learning process become principles of education. Technique A produces result C, and technique B produces result C. A choice can be made between A and B if C is desired. If, because of some value of education, A is undesirable and B is neutral, B is the principle of education that should be adopted.

Notice that in this model both value statements and educational principles are expressed as "should" statements because both stress values. The learning principles are in essence "is" statements, having to do with undisputed facts. It is important to remember, however, that values in education are real in that they do exist.

TABLE II.1

Learning Principles	Educational Values	Educational Principle
A produces C. B produces C.	C should be produced. A should be avoided.	The teacher should use B to produce C.

They differ from other varieties of facts in their origin. Values in education may range all the way from the value "Children should not be subjected to unnecessary stress" to the value "Children should learn history." The curriculum of the school is actually the manifestation of a value system. It states, in effect, that students should learn this content rather than some other content.

The illustration is based on a "fact" from psychology, but the model would be the same were the contributing discipline sociology, economics, or some other field. Depending upon the empirical data used and the value system applied, the resultant educational principle might vary from a recommendation for the color of chalk boards to a recommendation for particular legislation in the interest of education. Because all of the questions related to education are the result of one central concern, the model is applicable to all problems of education. Since our present concern is the Teaching-Learning Process, we will use the model primarily for viewing the development of principles of education from principles of behavior.

In education there is a lack of agreement on many of the values that must be considered in forming principles of education. One school may value one aspect of learning while another may not. The application of different value systems will lead to different principles of education. The educator must form principles of education on the basis of the data of learning or principles of sociology or the contributions of any discipline together with the value system to which he is committed.

A principle of education will not necessarily be a specific method of teaching; it may be a generic ideal that can be met by more than one classroom procedure. To illustrate, it is known that "punishment" reduces the probability that *all* preceding responses will occur again. Consider the child who volunteers an answer in class and is wrong. The problem is to let him know that he is wrong without reducing his interest and his tendency to volunteer later. The general education principle would be to inform the child he is wrong in a way that separates the wrong response from the act of volunteering. The model for this principle is shown in Table II.2.

The principle of education presented in Table II.2 does not indicate how it can be invoked. There is more than one technique that may be used to achieve the ends of the principle. To extend the model into the realm of classroom practice, it is necessary to include some other considerations. Of the many potentially valid techniques, some will be eliminated because of restrictions inherent in a particular teacher. Any one teacher because of skill, personality, or interest may be unable to use some techniques while another teacher could use them and not be able to use others. Similar restrictions are imposed by the nature of the learner. Techniques that will work with one child will not work with another because of ability, interests, motivation, or personality. In addition, some techniques will be eliminated because of economic and administrative realities. The class may be too large for some techniques, special equipment may be too expensive, or time may be limited. Table II.3 illustrates the extension of the model into the realm of practice.

The combined model—Tables II.1, II.2, and II.3—presents the considerations that are important in making decisions about how to teach. These considerations include facts of learning, values of education, principles of education, teacher variables, learner variables, and practical realities.

In many instances the model will be simplified. Suppose we have as facts that children can learn the explanation of eclipses through a particular teaching procedure and that no known procedure is superior. That they do learn about eclipses by this method is a fact. Values enter when we decide whether they should learn about eclipses rather than about something else. If learning about eclipses is valued, then this method will be used. This exam-

TABLE II.2

Learning Principle	Educational Values	Educational Principle
"Punishment" reduces the probability that all preceding responses will occur again.	Wrong responses should be eliminated. Volunteering is desirable.	The teacher should inform the child he is wrong by a technique that does not reduce the tendency to volunteer.

TABLE II.3

Educational Principle	Potential Techniques	Teacher Restrictions
P	T_1 T_2 T_3 T_4 T_5 T_6 T_7	T_1 and T_2 eliminated because teacher lacks special skills. T_4 eliminated because of conflict with teacher's personality.

ple is given as an instance where the facts used to develop a principle of education may be discovered, evaluated, and employed entirely within the discipline of education. But whether the empirical data comes from within education or from another source, the involvement of educational values makes the resultant principle uniquely part of the discipline of education.

A MODEL FOR FORMING RESEARCH HYPOTHESES IN EDUCATION

Hypotheses for educational research can be generated by a model quite similar to the model used in forming principles of education. Of all the hypotheses that could be tested, only those which are compatible with any particular value system in education need to be tested. If the interest was in behavior in general, then many more hypotheses could be explored. If it is known that variables A and B are correlated, the scientist might be equally interested in discovering whether the introduction of A produces B as he is in discovering whether the introduction of B can produce A. But if the educator values only B and is neutral toward A, he

TABLE II.4

Empirical Fact	Educational Values	Educational Hypothesis
A and B are correlated.	A is neutral. B is desirable.	Will the introduction of A produce B?

Learner Restrictions	Administrative and Economic Restrictions	Decision for Action
Maturity of child eliminates T_6. Ability of child eliminates T_5.	T_7 is too expensive.	T_3 should be used to fulfill educational principle P.

will be interested only in exploring the hypothesis that introducing A can produce B. Table II.4 shows the model for hypothesis choice in this case. The educator does not test the hypothesis that the introduction of B may produce A, because even if it does, the result is not of value to his concern.

Or, suppose the problem is more complex, as shown in Table II.5. In this example the educator will not test the hypothesis that the institution of A may produce B because his values dictate that he will not use A even if the hypothesis is true.

The model may be extended in many ways. For example, there may be hierarchies of values. In some instances it may not be possible to realize some value without foregoing another. The problem would then become one of the value of the values, and the lesser value would be sacrificed. If I value children learning a particular body of knowledge and I also value not producing

TABLE II.5

Empirical Facts	Educational Values	Educational Hypothesis
1) A and B are correlated. 2) C and B are correlated. 3) A and C are not correlated.	B is desirable. A is undesirable. C is neutral.	Will the introduction of C produce B?

anxiety in the classroom, a problem arises if learning this body of knowledge automatically produces anxiety. In that case I, as a teacher, must decide which value should be realized and be prepared to pay the cost of losing the other value. Decision making, then, is a central skill of teaching.

In the next section we will consider the empirical facts of learning and how they, together with educational values, lead to general principles of education. Later we will discuss ways in which the individual learner and teacher can influence the choice of teaching techniques.

•

CHAPTER THREE

Some Empirical Aspects

of Teaching and Learning

in the Classroom

•

There are many aspects of learning that we know very little about. This is especially true of those processes assumed to operate in the brain and the rest of the central nervous system. The question of how knowledge is stored, for example, has not yet been answered. Speculation has included the possibility that learning consists of changes in the membrane of some nerve cell, that there is some change in the electrical characteristics of certain nerve fibers, or that electrical fields in the brain as a whole are altered. Recently there has been speculation that information may be stored in the brain in the form of specially coded protein molecules, a notion similar to that used to explain the inheritance of genetic characteristics through protein molecules carrying the necessary information located in the individual's chromosomes.

Another unsolved question is that of how we locate and retrieve the information stored in our brain when we need it. If we need a certain book in a library, we go to the card catalog, locate the alphabetically placed card, and use the call number to find the book on the shelf. But if a person is asked a question about cars, houses, names, or any other topic, he can quickly produce what he knows about the subject. In this case, unlike the use of the library, we do not know by what process the stored information was located and made explicit.

Scientists who study the mind hope to be able to answer these questions eventually. But in the meantime we must work with what we do know. A fair amount is known about the relation between input and output—that is, between those antecedent variables which can be measured and changes in behavior. In the classroom, the question might be put in the form: What experiences will result in the student learning what the teacher wants him to learn? We can study the relationship between various ways of teaching and the results each produce even though we do not know many aspects of what happens "inside" the learner. Perhaps the situation is not unlike that of the first farmers who found that fertilizer produced better crops. Their lack of knowledge about the biochemistry of plants did not prevent them from making use of the discovery. It is true, of course, that developments in biochemistry led to superior crop yields, and in the same manner increased knowledge of the nature of learning may lead to superior techniques of instruction in the future.

As we discussed earlier, it is not sufficient for the educator merely to know the empirical correlates of learning. He must evaluate this information in terms of a value system in order to determine its relevance for the classroom teaching-learning process.

THE DYNAMICS OF CLASSROOM LEARNING

People can acquire knowledge and skills as the result of quite diverse activities. Often learning is the result of an individual's intention to master and retain specific material. When an older student uses flash cards to learn a foreign language vocabulary, or a younger child requests a parent to hear him spell the words assigned for the week, attention is specifically directed toward the acquisition of definite knowledge. When there is sufficient intrinsic motivation to acquire particular knowledge or a particular skill, acquisition is the goal of learning and also its reward.

At other times, learning takes place as the result of trying to attain some goal that for the learner is not related in any obvious way to learning. Learning can, then, be the by-product of activities in which there is no conscious intention to learn *per se* but where learning is required to reach the goal. When the motivation for activity is completely based on the goal, there is always the possibility that an alternative route will be found that bypasses specific learning. If a child wishes to be able to read, the only way he can acquire this skill is by learning to read. However, if he desires to read in order to gain the approval of his parents or the teacher, he may attempt to find a less demanding route. The goal of gaining approval is extrinsic to the learning of reading, and the student may try to gain the coveted approval by changing his social behavior or by using some other technique which avoids the necessity of learning.

There seems to be a third way in which learning occurs— incidental acquisition as the by-product of engaging in an activity, even though learning is neither intentional nor necessary to the activity. The acquisition of attitudes is typically based on this form of learning. For example, two students may acquire certain skills in mathematics, but one student may also acquire positive attitudes toward the subject while the other student may form negative attitudes. Two different teaching techniques may lead to the same goal, but differ in the effects which they produce.

Attitudes are not the only example of incidental learning. Many trivial aspects of the environment may be remembered, but usually only for a short time. We can recall what we had for lunch earlier in the day and may even remember seeing a particular person across the room. These items were retained without intention, and their learning was not essential to the pursuit of any recognizable goal. These last examples seem to illustrate that some forms of learning require only that the individual pay attention to some feature of his surroundings. What is learned is soon forgotten, because it is not applied or rehearsed. For this reason, most incidental learning is of little relevance to the teaching-learning process. Attitudes, however, are very important because they have an enduring effect upon the learner's actions.

All three of these ways in which learning occurs are of concern to the teacher. Most of the learning that takes place in the classroom cannot be classified without some ambiguity, but usually one form or another is predominant. Let us first consider the determinants of learning in the classroom.

REINFORCEMENT FOR LEARNING IN THE CLASSROOM

The rate of learning is determined by many factors, including the ability of the students, their motivation, and the nature of learning itself. The questions of motivation, the ability to learn, and other considerations will be discussed later; here we will consider the nature of learning as a phenomenon. In other words, we shall for the moment assume that the learners have the ability to acquire what is taught and that the teacher can provide positive reinforcement—otherwise there would be little or no learning. Another way of presenting the present question is to ask, "What determines the nature and rate of learning when it does in fact occur?" Stating the problem this way separates it from the issue of what the prerequisites of learning are.

The nature of the material to be learned is usually the most important single factor in determining the course of learning. The more meaningful the material is to the learner, the simpler it is to learn. We shall reserve discussion of meaningfulness for the next chapter.

In the following discussion the term *reinforcement* will be used as a convenient way of labeling certain stimuli which have been found to facilitate learning, including both the teacher's reactions to a student's performance and the student's own reactions. By reinforcement as used here we mean "feedback." The use of the term *reinforcement* should not be interpreted as the adoption of any particular learning theory. As was discussed earlier, there is no agreement on the function of reinforcement *qua* reinforcement in the production of learning. However, it is agreed that when a student's performance leads to certain consequences, there is an effect upon that performance in the future.

When a response is followed by positive reinforcement, the probability that the response will occur again is increased. The more often a response is followed by positive reinforcement, the greater is the probability of its being produced under the same circumstances. There is, then, a cumulative effect of positive reinforcement. A person is said to have learned when there is a very high probability that under certain conditions he will produce the correct response.

One problem in the evaluation of learning is the criteria of learning. Has a person learned a poem when he can recite it once without error, or twice, or is there some other standard? The usual criterion of learning is a high probability of the response being correct, but the exact standard is typically subjective and will vary from teacher to teacher. Unfortunately, there are few measures of the effect of what is learned in the classroom on behavior outside the classroom. The teacher tends to judge that a student has learned when he gives a correct answer either in discussion or on a test. This one-shot measure tells nothing about long-term retention, or about whether the learning has any meaning for the student when the school day is over. Nor is it always true that learning is correlated with later income and career choice. People who get the best employment are often chosen because they have been in school longer, not because they have learned more. Time in school *per se* becomes a prerequisite because it is assumed that the more schooling a person has, the more he knows. This assumption is often unwarranted. One need only look at the lack of competence in writing and speaking their own language that is typical of most students after twelve years of formal training in the schools.

Most of the "rewards" for correct responses that the teacher can provide are rewarding because the students have learned to value them, i.e., they are *secondary rewards*. Typically, approval and praise make up the majority of the positive reinforcement provided by the teacher. "That is right," "good," and "very good" probably account for most of the verbal approval received by an individual during his school experience. The same words are often written on work papers, or check marks are used. The check mark is interesting because it is in itself a very abstract symbol; yet it quickly comes to represent approval, much as an X represents disapproval.

Being allowed to engage in some desired activity is another positive reinforcement. When the student who correctly completes his desk work is permitted to read a book, or to start an art project, there is a double reinforcement—the implicit approval of the teacher and the privilege of reading the book or working on the art project. Another type of positive reinforcement is allowing the student to read his essay to the class or to post his work in the room. This type of reinforcement combines approval with other social rewards.

Social rewards do more than satisfy social needs; they also permit the individual to reward himself. Whenever a student's self-esteem is raised, he will be more likely to repeat the actions which brought him to that state. Often the young learner is not confident about the adequacy of his performance. When he is told that what he has done is good, his anxiety is reduced and learning is facilitated. It is very important that the student learn to reward himself; for if an individual is completely dependent upon social rewards as "social" rewards rather than as information, he will be at a loss when they are absent. The college student does not receive the social rewards for correct responses that are carefully given to the elementary-school child. He must be able, in effect, to reward himself by perceiving the success of his efforts. In the large university, the student who comes from a small rural high school is sometimes at a disadvantage in comparison to the student from a large urban high school. The latter student has already faced the problem of not receiving special rewards for every correct response and has learned to reward himself. Thus he is less dependent upon the social rewards possible with a close teacher-student relationship.

The teacher can help the younger student in the development of self-reinforcement. When a child is told "You should be very pleased with yourself" or "Doesn't that make you feel happy that you did it right?" stress is placed on the importance of self-actualization and inner-determined standards and rewards. If a student believes that he is capable of good work, he is rewarded by any feedback that confirms this hypothesis. The student with lower self-esteem may be surprised at first by rewards, but in time he will gain an improved self-image that will allow him to think that his efforts are worth while. When people reach the state of believing that they are capable of quality productions, external rewards become less critical, and the ability to judge the merit of performance becomes more internalized.

Disapproval in the classroom usually takes the form of a statement containing the word *no*, as in "No, that is not right," or the withholding of positive reinforcement. When an individual expects positive reinforcement, its absence is interpreted as disapproval and to some extent has the effect of punishment. It is important that the disapproval be attached to the wrong response and not be allowed to generalize. Negative feedback should not be allowed to lower self-esteem or to influence other desirable behavior, e.g., willingness to volunteer an answer. Different techniques will appeal to the personalities of different teachers, but each technique must in some way provide positive reinforcement for correct responses if it is to succeed in the production of learning. One way in which this can be done is by guiding the student to the point where he realizes why he was wrong and then giving him positive reinforcement for his insight. The following exchange between a teacher and student is illustrative:

> Teacher: "Will people be able to talk to one another on the moon in the same way that they do on earth?"
> Tom: (who has raised his hand and has been chosen by the teacher to answer the question): "Yes, the same language will work just as well there as here."
> Teacher: "Is there any difference between the air here and on the moon?"
> Tom: "Yes, on the moon there is no air. Oh, I see now; there would be nothing to carry their voices. I guess men on the moon would have to use radios.
> Teacher: "Very good, Tom. That is right."

In this example, the teacher assisted the student in reaching the right answer. What could have been nothing more than a failure experience has been converted into a successful interaction. The way in which it was done permits the student to take credit for the success. He has learned the important point and will willingly volunteer again.

The feedback received by the learner brings about modifications in his performance. No matter how long a person practices with a typewriter, there will be no real improvement if he cannot see the results of his efforts. In one experiment, individuals were instructed to draw a line four inches in length. They were then asked to try again many times but were given no information as to their accuracy. Their last attempts were no more accurate than their first, illustrating that practice alone, without feedback, does not result in learning. One of the major tasks of the teacher is to provide feedback to the students so that they can adjust their performance.

The lack of immediate feedback is one of the great weaknesses of most homework assignments. The student completes the assignment and then turns to some desired activity. He has, in effect, been reinforced for what he has done whether it is right or wrong. When he learns the next day, or often later, that part of his performance was incorrect, there is little or no negative evaluation of the specific errors; instead, a negative atmosphere generalizes to homework in general. Another disadvantage of homework is that it has to compete with very desirable alternatives. The student must stop some enjoyable activity in order to do homework, and he knows that the sooner the work is done, the sooner he can turn to more pleasant pursuits. The fact that the teacher is responsible for this chore contributes to many students' dislike of school. In view of both the lack of feedback and the engendering of negative attitudes, there is some real doubt about the merit of homework in the early years of schooling.

Feedback need not always be purely verbal. Often demonstrations and experiments permit students to observe the adequacy of their hypotheses. In a physics class, students may be asked for their opinion of the results of evacuating the air from a tin can. If the experiment is conducted after they have made their predictions, the results will provide feedback to both those who were right and those who were in error. One advantage of this and related techniques is that it takes the teacher out of the role of being the sole source of reinforcement. A similar result is achieved when a student is given the task of finding the solution to some problem that has been discussed in class and reporting his findings to the group.

The attitudes that students form toward a teacher are determined, in part, by the teacher's role in the education process. To the extent that students have an opportunity to assume aspects of that role, they can develop an understanding of the two sides of the teaching-learning process. There also exists here the possibility of arousing interest in teaching as a profession. There is no reason why students should not be given many more opportunities to function as teachers than is typically permitted. Teaching a body of material to a group gives the student a greater understanding of the content and relationships than is achieved when he is merely assigned the task of learning it. In addition, the assumption of the teaching role provides practice in leadership and self-expression.

The teacher does not always have to wait for the desired response to be completed before giving a reward. Research has clearly demonstrated that it is possible to "shape" behavior by giving rewards for components or approximations of the desired performance. Thus, when a student is on the right track, he may be told "good" or "yes, can you tell us more?" Often a student may know the correct response, but lack confidence. If his partially correct response does not result in any feedback, he is very likely to assume that he is wrong. By giving some reward for partially correct responses, the teacher both builds up the self-confidence of the learner and prevents him from excessive trial and error. Approval for responses that approach the desired goal also reduces the probability that slower students will have a totally negative experience in the classroom. Often a nod from the teacher at the right moment is quite sufficient feedback, and the student proceeds with increased confidence. The teacher must be careful, however, to avoid the easy assumption that cues which are obvious to him are equally obvious to the young learner.

It is important for a person to learn to monitor his own behavior and appreciate that he is making progress toward his goal. Often a goal is far removed in time, and if there are no rewards along the way, the individual may abandon goal-oriented behavior. Once he has learned to appreciate partial achievement, his progress toward the goal will be maintained. This capacity becomes even more critical when the child grows up because an adult must often devote energy to activities for which the reward is remote. Since children usually lack the capacity to work for very distant goals, they must be given goals which are within reach, and the teacher should reward fairly small steps. The fact that young children are easily discouraged may be understood in terms of their inability to work without external incentives for long durations.

The student can also receive feedback from the rest of the class. Anyone who has ever taught or observed a class in progress has witnessed what happens when a student gives a response that many other members of the group know is wrong or lacking in some important manner. Instantly, many hands are raised, which say, in effect, "That is not right. I know the answer." The student soon begins to take this group behavior as evidence that he should alter his response or someone else will be given a chance to respond. When he gives the answer that the others had in mind, their hands are lowered, and he takes this as evidence that he has successfully coped with the problem. The fact that others seem to have the right answer also serves to prompt the individual to expend more energy himself. Feedback from the rest of the class is also possible when students work on a project or experiment in groups because other members of the group can directly endorse or criticize the productions of an individual.

The objectives of education are most likely to be realized when reinforcement, or feedback, comes from individuals whom the learner holds in esteem. When the teacher is esteemed, his task is greatly simplified. But all too often students do not value the teacher's approval and may even view rewards from the teacher as a dangerous threat to their peer-group relationships. Sometimes the teacher must overcome attitudes formed in the home or during unfortunate earlier experiences in school. When this is accomplished, the teacher can more successfully reward students for their efforts. However, if there is no other source of reinforcement, there can be unfortunate consequences. When rewards become commonplace and are always of the same form, interest soon wanes and the individual turns his attention elsewhere. There is also always the danger that the person may come to depend upon particular rewards or a specific form of feedback; to that extent, he will be lost without it.

It may be that we could pay students to learn, and they would in fact learn specific material in return for financial remuneration. Even if the funds were available, it is obvious that the practice could not be permitted, for it would conflict with some of the basic values of the school—for instance, that people should come to desire knowledge for many of its intrinsic rewards, not for a specific "pay-off." It is true that extrinsic rewards are often used, but these differ from a financial reward in their effect upon the individual. When a person enjoys a task because others are participating with him, the activity has social rewards in addition to whatever intrinsic value it may have. Money would be an extrinsic reward too, but the effect upon the individual's attitude toward the task would be quite different from that generated by social reinforcement. In addition, when a person works for money, the concrete reward tends to dominate as a goal, and when there is no longer any remuneration, he ceases to pursue the activity. On the other hand, social rewards can often serve to maintain an activity until the individual reaches a point where he is actually reinforcing himself through increased self-esteem and from the intrinsic aspects of the activity. Perhaps it is because social rewards are more subtle that they are less likely to become the focus of attention, even though they have at least as much value to the individual as other forms of reinforcement. When a person is engaged in an activity for money, he has very explicit knowledge of why he is working. A person may, however, continue to engage in an activity because of social reinforcement without the reinforcement dominating his attention, thereby allowing him to discover other sources of reward inherent in the activity.

REINFORCEMENT AND THE MAINTENANCE OF BEHAVIOR

Thus far, we have directed attention to the relationship between learning and reinforcement, or feedback. As was stated earlier, such an emphasis may be misleading, and it would be wise at this time to approach classroom learning with a different frame of reference. In the last analysis, what the teacher sees and can work with is the performance, the behavior, of the students. Usually, when there is an improvement in the performance of a learner, he is said to have "learned." (We know this is not necessarily the case; sometimes performance improves because of increased motivation without additional learning.) Learning may be regarded as a by-product of performance; when performance changes, feedback informs the individual about the results of his efforts.

Viewing the problem in this way permits us to raise a new question. What is the relation between reinforcement, or feedback, and the maintenance of performance? It is possible to study this phenomenon without bringing up the issue of learning. A man may go to work every day and engage in some activity that results in no further learning. For example, one could, in a routine factory job, reach a level of performance which would remain constant. The level of performance would be maintained without further learning. What caused the performance to be maintained? The constant performance constituted a rehearsal of the skill. In the classroom there are many activities that represent rehearsal of what has already been learned. Writing, reading, and the use of new vocabulary in discussions are but a few examples. Thus, practice maintains the skills that are essential for the acquisition of new material. Much of the content material taught in the schools receives little rehearsal and is soon forgotten. Fortunately, the basic academic skills and essential nonacademic social skills do receive considerable emphasis every day in the better classrooms.

Naturally, the teacher is most concerned with the kind of performance that results in learning, but for the moment let us look at some of the determinants of performance in general. Some incentives are far more effective than others for the production of activity and the maintenance of performance. In Chapter Five, we will give intensive consideration to the role of motivation and will treat the relative efficacy of various goals. At the moment, we will direct our attention to the relationship between the frequency of reinforcement and the rate of performance.

The activity of an individual is not constant over time. Sometimes a person will work with great energy on some project while at other times there will be no activity. A wealth of experimental data has demonstrated that there is a relationship between the performance of an organism and the reinforcement that is received for performance. Most of the research has been conducted using animals, usually rats or pigeons, under highly controlled laboratory conditions. Because of this, many of the conclusions may have few implications for the classroom, but there are some parallels worthy of attention.

SCHEDULES OF REINFORCEMENT

One relationship between performance and reinforcement for that performance is referred to as the *schedule of reinforcement*. If reinforcement occurred with every performance, it would be *100 per cent*, or *continuous reinforcement*. Usually, however, reinforcement does not occur every time the correct response is given. This would be classified as *partial reinforcement*, of which there are several types.

Consider a man who works in a factory and has the job of putting rivets into certain units that are produced. There is more than one way in which he can be paid for this work. He might be paid a fixed amount at the end of the week as long as his work was "satisfactory" by some criteria. In practice, he would be expected to complete some minimum number of units. If, however, he is on piece work and is paid an amount for every ten units he completes, the schedule of reinforcement is very different.

The pay system that rewards some minimum productivity during a preceding time period represents a *fixed minimum* schedule of reinforcement (such as the man who is paid weekly). The man who is paid for completing a certain number of units is receiving reinforcement on a *fixed ratio* schedule. These different reinforcement schedules will not maintain performance at the same level. The fixed ratio schedule usually produces a high rate of performance, while the fixed minimum schedule often maintains behavior at the lowest adequate level.

The schedule of reinforcement can also determine the manner in which performance is distributed over time as well as exerting an effect on the average rate of performance. With a fixed minimum schedule of reinforcement, the performance required to obtain the reinforcement will often occur immediately before the reinforcement is due, instead of being distributed equally over the time interval between reinforcements. One example is the behavior of many students when they know that a term paper will be due by a certain date. They often delay the work as long as possible and then find themselves laboring late into the night before the deadline. The same is true of exams; many students cram their studying into the days immediately before the exam rather than distributing the effort over time.

Another schedule of reinforcement is based on *fixed intervals.* A rat can be trained to push a lever to obtain food with the reward coming only if he presses the lever after a fixed interval of time. If the interval is one minute, no responses are rewarded until a minute has passed, and then the first response after that time is reinforced by food. This schedule appears at first to be very similar to the fixed minimum schedule, but there are critical differences. With the fixed minimum schedule the essential responses must all occur before some deadline. The fixed interval schedule rewards the first response that occurs after the deadline and rewards none of the responses that occur earlier. Under a fixed interval schedule the rat learns to restrain from further responding for a period immediately following a reward. It learns not to respond again until the time interval has passed.

There seem to be very few examples of the use of fixed interval schedules in the classroom. An example would have to show that reward only followed responses given after a time interval and not before. The child who shouts out an answer and is not rewarded because he did not wait for the teacher to call on him would not be a case in point because here it is a signal from the teacher that is critical and not the passage of a time interval alone. One example of fixed interval reinforcement occurs in reading aloud. The child must learn to pause at commas and periods, or he will not be praised by the teacher. If he starts the next sentence without that critical pause, there is no reward. The case just given is obviously strained and illustrates the fact that many learning situations which can be studied in the laboratory are quite artificial when applied to the classroom.

Another variety of partial reinforcement is *random reinforcement* where it is impossible to predict whether or not a given response will be reinforced. Sometimes reinforcement occurs while other times it does not. Reinforcement may occur often, for example 80 per cent of the time, or seldom, perhaps following only 5 per cent of the units of performance. Consider a group of artists who differ in talent and as a result vary in success when they attempt to sell a painting. One artist may sell most of his productions while another sells very few. Both men receive partial reinforcement for painting, and reinforcement is random to the extent that they do not know whether or not any given production will sell. There are other specific reinforcement schedules of particular interest to the laboratory investigator, but the ones just introduced are the schedules that have relevance for performance in the classroom.

REINFORCEMENT SCHEDULES AND CLASSROOM PERFORMANCE

Because we are concerned with the behavior of people, the effect on classroom performance of using a particular reinforcement schedule is not as predictable as it is with lower organisms in a controlled experiment. One basic problem is that it is often very difficult to know exactly what reinforcement schedule is in operation or, for that matter, how many reinforcement systems are functioning at the same time. A student may, for example, be receiving some form of partial reinforcement from the teacher while he is receiving continuous reinforcement from some other source. This would occur if a teacher told a student "good" following some of his correct responses, but the student learned in other ways that he was correct most of the time. One instance in which this operates is when the teacher poses questions to the class and then calls upon individuals for their responses. Even though a student is not selected to answer, he learns whether or not the response he had formed was correct from the teacher's reaction to some other student's reply. The satisfaction of knowing he had the answer results in a higher rate of reinforcement than that which would be identified from considering only how often he was called upon and was correct in his response.

People learn to mediate between the event of one major reinforcement and the next by supplying themselves with symbolic reinforcements that are difficult to analyze. When a person is working toward some goal, he tells himself at each step that he is closer, and in this way he provides himself with reinforcement that can maintain his performance over long periods. Or, a man may have a job that he does not like, but continue to work because he can think about what he will do with the money, even though he will not be paid in the immediate future. His thought about the reward can, in effect, temporarily substitute for the reward in the reinforcement of his performance.

Even though no reinforcement schedule operates in isolation from other sources of reinforcement in the classroom, some schedules used by the teacher do produce a noticeable effect. When students are set a task, for example an arithmetic problem or writing exercise that must be completed by a certain time, their behavior is typical of fixed minimum schedules. Some members of the class will be aware that they have been allotted considerably more time than they need. These students are usually more advanced than most of the class and have learned from past experience that they can accomplish classroom assignments in less time than the rest. Knowing that they have more than sufficient time, these students will often not start to work immediately but instead will allow themselves to be diverted by what others are doing or by random activity and daydreaming. Or, they may start to work slowly and with little effort, being easily diverted from their task. Suddenly they realize that they have miscalculated and time is running out. The tasks are completed, or partially completed, in great haste with the obvious consequence that quality suffers and little is learned.

Another schedule of reinforcement can avoid some of these problems. The teacher will achieve quite different results with the use of a modified fixed ratio schedule. Instead of setting a fixed time for the completion of the task, the teacher could reward completion of the task with the restriction that the work must also reach a certain level of quality. For example, the students may be told that as soon as they are finished they should bring their papers to the teacher to be checked. When a student has completed his desk work, he is allowed to select a book to read or perhaps a number game or puzzle which he can use at his desk while the others are still working. At first, some of the learners will rush through the assigned task with completion as their only goal, but they soon learn that this is not enough. After the teacher has sent them back to their desks a few times to correct the results of hasty effort, the students learn that the only successful strategy is to work both steadily and carefully.

It is important to note that the teacher should not reward output without regard to quality. The use of a joint criterion permits the encouragement of both high productivity and high quality. The students soon learn the criteria set by the teacher and use these criteria to monitor their own efforts. The teacher must raise the criteria of quality if he expects the students to produce at increasingly higher levels. Each increase in the criteria must be large enough that the students can distinguish it from the previously acceptable level, but small enough to be a reasonably obtainable goal. If the required level of performance is set too high, frustration will result, and the students may decide that the reward is not worth the effort. Students will differ in the size of the improvement increment that they can handle, and there is no reason why the teacher should impose the same new criteria on all. Experience with the individual members of the class will reveal to the teacher the level at which the next goal should be placed.

Random reinforcement can also maintain performance at a high level. While students are working individually on an art project or cursive writing exercise, the teacher may walk about the room, going from desk to desk. Sometimes the teacher may say to an individual "very good," or give some suggestion for improvement, or have the student hold up his work so that the rest of the class can see the fine results. If everyone received the same reward every time the teacher stopped at their desks, there would be less reason for effort. The knowledge that there is some degree of uncertainty is not only realistic but essential: people do not work with great effort if they begin to believe that they will be rewarded no matter what they do. This is especially true of young students who do not yet possess a highly developed capacity for self-reinforcement.

Uncertainty about whether or not a reward will be received generates some degree of anxiety in an individual. There is evidence that anxiety is not categorically bad and, indeed, can be of benefit under certain circumstances. When a student decides to study rather than go to the movies, he is often motivated by tension produced by an impending exam. Without this mild anxiety he might well decide to do something other than study. Tranquilizers have been known to cause people to fail to prepare for some important event, an exam or a speech, because all tension was removed.

The anxiety that causes a student to prepare or exert effort in class is quite different from the anxiety of the student waiting for his grade after the test is over. The latter anxiety is dysfunctional; it serves no constructive motivational purpose. Although dysfunctional anxiety (anxiety which is sufficiently severe to disrupt performance) should be avoided, some degree of tension is usually a prerequisite for adequate functioning. Besides motivating performance, mild tension facilitates performance while it is occurring. People do not perform at their best when completely "relaxed." For each type of task, and for each individual, there seems to be some optimal level of tension at which performance is at its highest.

STUDENT-SET REINFORCEMENT SCHEDULES

Beyond the elementary school years, the teacher has little opportunity to use schedules of reinforcement in the classroom, other than by providing positive feedback to as many individuals as possible during the short class session. (Remember that beyond the sixth year of school, students move from teacher to teacher during the day and spend less than an hour with any one teacher.)

However, the teacher can exercise some control over the student's study activity even through the college years. For example, when the teacher or the college professor schedules a test or examination, or when some assignment is due, the student's study activity outside of school changes. Concentrated study right before a deadline is not optimal for learning, although some learning does occur. One reason why it is not optimal is that the distribution of practice has been shown to be related to the results of practice. When there is extreme concentration of practice over a short time span, referred to as *massed practice*, less learning results, and the retention of what is learned seems to be reduced. The same amount of practice over a longer period of time—*spaced practice*—is preferable. When studying, the student benefits from taking occasional "breaks" from the task. Forty-five minutes' study followed by a ten- or fifteen-minute break and then another forty-five minutes of study may produce more learning than two hours of uninterrupted concentration. The actual choice of length of practice and frequency and duration of "breaks" depends upon both the individual and the nature of the material or task. Experience should reveal to each learner what combination is optimal for him. There is evidence that length of practice is a more important variable than is length of the rest period. Beyond a relatively short time, there is little gain from extending the length of the work break.

Popular theories that attempt to explain the advantages of spaced practice over massed practice use the concept of *inhibition*. In essence, the notion is that work results in an inhibitory feedback that interferes with further work. The rest period gives this inhibitory potential an opportunity to dissipate. Inhibitory potential may be compared with the popular notion of fatigue. When a person becomes fatigued, he must rest for a short time or he will not be able to work effectively.

Older students learn to put themselves on schedules of reinforcement, but often they do not choose the criteria of success wisely. Many college students use study goals that are analogous to fixed minimum schedules. That is, they declare to themselves that they will study French vocabulary for two hours and then go to meet friends or engage in some other desirable activity. Often they can set this rule and adhere to it, but the problem is that there is no criterion for the quality of the study activity. Even though his attention may wander and the study is in general inefficient, the student is satisfied when the two hours are over, because he has accomplished his goal. The goal should, however, have been a different one, namely, the mastery of certain material. Using flash cards, the student can offer himself the same incentive but have as his goal learning the French equivalents of a predetermined number of English words. When he can produce the right response to each English word, he knows that he has reached his goal, and he *knows* exactly what he has learned. With this approach he has put himself on a ratio schedule which requires more than the mere passage of "time on the job." The problem remaining for the student is how to choose a realistic goal. If the goal is too easy to reach, little has been learned; while if the goal is unrealistically high, he may abandon the task and allow himself to receive the promised reward anyway. Once the latter occurs a few times, the student may gradually abandon what could have been a very effective study program.

As a result of experience, the individual must be willing to readjust his goals in order to maintain his performance. One way in which this may be done is by introducing the time criterion in a new context. Instead of studying for two hours, the student might select a goal that requires two hours. A moment's reflection reveals that these represent quite different tactics. If the goal requires far less than two hours' effort, or far more, the learner can change his goal accordingly the next time he studies.

Whole theories of personality and adjustment can be built on the problem of choosing realistic goals, and when individuals are very extreme in their choice of goals, the causes usually lie outside of the school and treatment may be beyond the resources of the classroom. Each individual maximizes both achievement and satisfaction when he works for the highest goals that he is capable of attaining. The term *under-achiever* has been used to designate those individuals whose achievements are lower than their measured potential would seem to permit. The *over-achiever* constantly strives to reach goals that would seem to be beyond his capacity. Occasionally he is successful as the result of prodigious effort and strain. However, it is a pace he cannot endure for very long. With underachievement, the result is a failure to make significant contributions to society, while at the other extreme, anxiety and frustration are produced. The teacher can be a significant influence in assisting students to set realistic goals. If the young learner is fortunate enough to have this guidance, he will avoid many problems in his future adjustment to schooling and general living.

In the preceding discussion the emphasis has been upon the maintenance of performance rather than upon the production of learning, even though the question of learning was occasionally reintroduced. The basic theme here is that when performance can be maintained, and when criteria are set for the quality of the performance, learning will occur. Learning has, by definition, occurred when performance quality improves under a constant level of motivation and reaches the standard or criteria set by the teacher or the learner himself. Having treated the relation between schedules of reinforcement and continuing performance, we are now ready to explore the relation between reinforcement schedules and the resistance of the performance level to change when reinforcement is no longer present.

REINFORCEMENT SCHEDULES AND EXTINCTION

The level of performance that is achieved as the result of reinforcement will change if the reinforcement is withdrawn. In general, when responses no longer result in positive reinforcement, they tend to occur less often. If reinforcement is not resumed, the rate of responding gradually returns to the operant rate of occurrence for that particular response. This *extinction* of behavior occurs at different rates for responses which have not had the same history of reinforcement. Although it seems paradoxical at first, performance which has had continuous or 100 per cent reinforcement is less resistant to extinction than performance which has had partial reinforcement.

An example may both illustrate the problem and lead to a resolution of the paradox. Consider two hypothetical students in an art class or in a shop course. Every time Tom completes a project, he is praised and told that it is very good, even though the quality may not be very high on several occasions. Bill, another student, is not praised for each accomplishment; instead he is sometimes praised and on other occasions receives no direct reinforcement. If reinforcement is withheld from both students, Bill, who in the past has received partial reinforcement for his efforts, will persevere in new attempts longer than will Tom with his history of continuous reinforcement.

The explanation for this phenomenon involves complexities beyond our purposes, but, in brief, there are two ways of thinking about the problem. One approach would be to point out that since Bill was not reinforced every time he performed in the past, the absence of reinforcement is not new or surprising. As far as he is concerned, this may be just one of the times that he receives no feedback, and so he goes on trying. For Tom, however, the sudden absence of reinforcement is surprising and devastating, and he soon gives up trying. With humans this explanation is adequate; however, animals respond in a similar manner even though their ability to reason is quite low. This gives rise to the second explanation which states that because the lack of reinforcement during extinction is more similar to partial reinforcement than to continuous reinforcement, performance maintained under partial reinforcement is more likely to be maintained during the absence of reinforcement. The first explanation assumes *conscious* mediation, the second does not.

For our purposes, it is sufficient to note that students can become dependent upon rewards if they expect them every time. When the rewards no longer occur, the effect on performance will be disruptive. This is especially true of younger students. With older students, rewards are likely to become commonplace and unattractive because of their high frequency. Because of their ability to reason, people often interpret the absence of reinforcement as punishment or rejection. For this reason, laboratory studies of the behavior of animals whose reinforcement is withdrawn can be misleading when extended into the realm of human reactions.

Even though partial reinforcement provides the greatest resistance to extinction, continuous reinforcement results in more rapid acquisition of new skills and more rapid improvement in the level of performance. It is possible to take advantage of the virtues of both reinforcement schedules and avoid the primary weaknesses of either one. In the early stages of learning, reinforcement should be as continuous as possible. (Note that this does not imply that the same form of reinforcement should be given every time; in fact, the form should be varied.) When, through the use of continuous reinforcement, performance has reached a high level, reinforcement may be given on a partial basis to make the performance more immune to extinction. In practice this progression normally occurs, because the teacher begins to pay reduced attention to praising fully acquired skills and concentrates on new learning, directing most of the reinforcement he has to offer in that direction.

Actually, extinction is not responsible for the loss of most skills or knowledge acquired in the classroom. There is really little opportunity for extinction to occur because the learned responses seldom are emitted without concomitant feedback. Many people learned Latin vocabulary that they cannot recall any longer. The reason that they can no longer give the correct response is obviously not due to giving it many times without reinforcement. Extinction and forgetting are different concepts and should not be equated. The only similarity is that the end result of both is the same—a person no longer makes responses or exhibits skills that he at one time possessed.

FORGETTING

Most people believe that the reason they have forgotten many facts and skills learned in school is that they have not used the information for many years. In essence, they believe that the sheer passage of time since they last used the information has produced the loss. For a long time, behavioral scientists concurred, and the theory of forgetting was based on the *principle of disuse*. The contemporary scientist is not satisfied with the use of time as a pure variable in the explanation of any phenomenon. He seeks the processes that account for the changes which superficially appear to be correlated only with the passage of time. Time may seem to cause iron to rust, but further investigation reveals the role of oxygen and its rate of combination with the iron.

INTERFERENCE THEORIES

The most widely held theories of forgetting use the concept of interference. The view is that certain response tendencies interfere with other responses and cause them to be unavailable to the individual. Later we will consider this problem as one facet of the transfer of learning and the interaction between new learning and old learning. In many ways interference theories of forgetting seem inadequate for explaining the forgetting of unique material, since there is apparently little related experience that could interfere. Interference theory shares the weakness of many behavioral theories in that it is almost impossible to prove wrong in the form in which it is stated. To show that an instance of forgetting was not due to interference, we would have to show that there was no interference with recall from any source, but we could never be positive that we had eliminated every possible source. There exists the equally unprovable notion that nothing, once learned, is ever forgotten. This view holds that through the use of association, hypnosis, or some other technique, recollection will occur. It is another example of an untestable hypothesis because one would have to prove that some items had been forgotten, and adherents to the concept would simply say that the right technique had not been found to produce recall.

REPRESSION AND SUPPRESSION

Some personality theories use the concept of *repression* to explain how information once known to the individual later becomes unavailable or "forgotten." According to the model, facts or ideas which are threatening to the person's self-esteem, or are in some other way unacceptable, are repressed or prevented from becoming conscious. Repression refers to the active restraint of certain information so that it will remain unconscious and takes place without the individual's conscious effort or knowledge. In contrast, *suppression* is the conscious, intentional act of withholding a response. If a person starts to speak but then has second thoughts about what he was going to say, he has suppressed the initial response and will perhaps substitute another. Suppression is permitted by the capacity of people for monitoring their own behavior. Repressed material becomes available, or conscious, to the individual, only if it loses its ego-threatening qualities. It is believed that there are wide individual differences in the tendency to employ repression in response to threatened self-esteem.

One alternative to the concept of repression is based on a learning model. The basic assumption is that thoughts are responses and, as such, are subject to modification by reinforcement or punishment. Those thoughts which produce anxiety are punished by that anxiety. Those responses (thoughts) which were responsible for the anxiety become less and less likely to occur. The individual can have these thoughts again once they no longer lead to anxiety, because responses return to the operant level of occurrence once punishment is removed.

It is not possible to give the concept of repression and the experimental evidence for its existence full justice here, but even if we assume the existence of the process, it seems to be of limited importance in the forgetting of classroom learning. Some related phenomena are of importance to education, and they may or may not involve the dynamics of repression. Unpleasant material is more difficult to learn than pleasant material, and it is not retained as well over time. This suggests no new considerations for the teacher but rather illustrates one of the many unfortunate consequences when the learner develops negative attitudes toward the content of a school subject.

PRACTICE AND REHEARSAL

Actually it is difficult to pinpoint the source of differential retention because data on practice and rehearsal are usually absent. Often a person will recite a long poem that he learned in school many years ago. Those present will compliment him on his fine memory, and the performer himself is usually convinced that he possesses an exceptional skill. What is important here is not how long it has been since he learned the poem but rather how long it has been since the last time he recited it. Some people time and time again display early learning as evidence of their good memory and never stop to think that each time they perform, they are giving themselves additional practice.

The same situation exists in the school; some material is rehearsed continuously while other information is seldom used. Once a child has learned to read or write, he receives additional practice the rest of his life, while information acquired in a history class may receive no rehearsal after the original learning. Once a skill has been acquired, subsequent practice will preserve it from loss due to interference or other factors. For example, it would probably require relatively little practice, with cooperation from parents, to prevent the loss in skills that young students undergo during summer vacation. While disuse does not *cause* loss of retention, it does *permit* the loss.

In addition to the history of spaced rehearsal, there is variation in the amount of original practice at the time of learning different material. Some skills and information are overlearned. That is, after they were learned, the individual continued to practice, and, as a result, the material is less subject to forgetting. The optimal amount of overlearning depends upon so many factors that firm principles have not yet been established. With older students, the claim has been made that 50 per cent overlearning is optimal, since beyond that, there are rapidly diminishing returns for extra effort. Fifty per cent overlearning would mean that if it took two hours to master some material, one would rehearse for an additional hour. The successful student learns by trial and error what he requires by way of rehearsal following learning, and the figures given above should not be taken as correct in any absolute sense.

THE DISTORTION OF RECALL BY VALUES AND PREDISPOSITIONS

Once material has been learned, factors other than extinction or forgetting may operate to make recall less than perfect. There is evidence that an individual's values may distort memory in a manner consistent with his value system. J. S. Bruner and C. C. Goodman have shown that poor children, when asked to duplicate the size of coins from memory, remember them as relatively larger than do children from affluent families.[1] Similarly, a child may remember a threatening individual as larger than he really was (there must have been some good reason for being frightened), and a big fish grows a bit larger each time the story is told and is only limited by one's arm span and the credulity of the audience.

Distortion of recall is a very serious problem in courts of law when testimony is given. Often a "leading" question will produce distortion that would not otherwise have occurred. In one testimony experiment a young lady suddenly appeared in the front of the classroom and, after a brief argument, drew out a water pistol, drenched the instructor, and departed.[2] As soon as the experimenter's accomplice had left, the class was asked to write a description of the sequence of events. The class was then asked several leading questions, including, "What color purse was she carrying?" Many of the witnesses indicated that there was a purse and gave its color, though in fact the young lady had not been carrying one. Through independent measures, the study demonstrated that those whose recall was distorted were individuals who tended to be acquiescent and also tended to monitor their behavior less than other people.

When people possess some plan or *schema* that they employ to organize their recall, distortion will occur to the extent that reality differs from the schema. One example can be seen with the prejudiced individual who organizes his recall of a situation involving minority group members in a manner compatible with his stereotypes. Apparently what actually happens is that the individual has many fragmentary memories which do not suffice to produce a coherent recollection. He draws upon other experiences which are organized into a schema and as a result "recalls" material that was not a part of the critical situation. If the person is prejudiced, his schemata will lead to verbal productions which reveal this bias. This does not mean that he perceived the situation wrong initially; rather, the bias occurred when he organized his memories for reproduction.

People employ many specific *social schemata* when they must deal with social situations. These schemata, which are aroused by the specific social content of the environment, determine the organization of behavior, but they can also lead to predictable errors. Some fundamental social schemata have been studied by using The Felt Figure Technique, in which human figures cut from felt are placed on a felt board.[3,4] Part of the technique involves judging the distance between two human figures. The subjects in the study first viewed the two figures presented with a fixed separation. The figures were then removed from the viewing field and handed to the subject who was told to replace them exactly as they were. People erred by replacing the human figures too close together, while their reconstruction of nonsocial displays was relatively accurate. The specific content of the pair of figures determines the magnitude of the error—for instance, a male-female figure pair are replaced closer together than two male figures or two female figures. Specific schemata exert an influence on behavior, whether verbal or nonverbal, visual or nonvisual. The Gestalt psychologists were often concerned with distortion of memory, especially in the area of visual perception, but worked mainly with simple geometric configurations. A great number of experiments were performed, accompanied by an elaborate theoretical system. Their studies cannot be fruitfully explored here, but the names of the central figures were mentioned in Chapter One (p. 29).

SELECTIVE RECALL

While recall is often distorted, it is at other times accurate, but selective—that is, the material that *is* recalled is not distorted, but other material is not recalled at all. People tend to recall facts with which they agree and have difficulty recalling material with which they disagree. Interrupted tasks are recalled to a greater extent than completed tasks.[5] One explanation may be that more attention is directed toward the uncompleted problem because of its greater challenge. This would, then, provide greater opportunities for incidental learning of various attributes of the task.

The typical research design has been to give people a set of tasks, some of which cannot be completed—since they have no solution. Each task has a name, and the subjects in the experiment are asked, at a later time, to recall as many of these names as possible. If the total situation is emotionally neutral, people tend to remember more of the names of problems they could not solve than of the ones they could complete. This tendency to recall uncompleted tasks is an example of selective recall. Personality variables interact with recall under these circumstances, and individuals do not respond consistently. When failure to complete the tasks is threatening to the ego of the individual, as when he is told that the tasks measure intelligence, he is more likely to be unable to recall the tasks which he did not complete.[6] This latter phenomenon may be repression.

Students will often show selective recall for material that is dramatic or humorous or that captures their attention for some other reason. The high school or college teacher soon learns that if he tells an amusing story to illustrate some point, he will receive the exact story, word for word, on examinations at the end of the term. The teacher must therefore take care to direct the students' attention to the most important aspects of the lesson. If trivia are dramatized or made interesting, trivia will be recalled later. In a way, the problem is similar to that which confronts the author when he writes a play. He does not want to direct attention to the wrong things because if he does, he may never recapture his audience. Successful teaching, like successful writing, occurs when peaks of attention are made to occur together with the central points, the important principles.

Recall is facilitated by the associative links between the material to be recalled and other material that has been learned. Often the recall of some material permits the recall of other memories. All of us have had the experience of suddenly recalling a "forgotten" name or incident because the recollection was triggered by some association, even though rather remote. Psychoanalysts and other therapists use the technique of association to help their patients recall events and ideas that occurred quite early in their lives. When a person attempts to recall a poem, he will start over if he has trouble because the associations aroused by the first lines aid him in recalling the rest. There are many examples of the facilitation of recall by associative cues.

Similarly, the student may be able to recall some physics principle by first recalling a classroom demonstration that was dramatic and then, by thinking about the demonstration, recall its objective. Material is meaningful to the extent that it is associatively linked to other material. Paul Johnson has shown that high school students who possess certain physics associations to physics words are more successful in the solution of physics problems than are students who lack these associations.[7]

A prime task of the teacher who wishes to teach for long retention is to make the material to be learned meaningful. How this may be accomplished and the relevance of meaningfulness to the total teaching-learning process is our next concern.

•

CHAPTER FOUR

Meaningfulness

and the

Transfer of Learning

•

THE LEARNING OF MEANINGFUL MATERIAL

What distinguishes meaningful material from material that is less meaningful? Certainly one distinguishing characteristic is familiarity—material is meaningful to the extent that it is related to, or associated with, something already known and understood. The greater the number of associations an item arouses, the more meaningful it will be.

FAMILIARITY AND THE MEANINGFULNESS OF MATERIAL

Familiarity can take many forms. Some material is meaningful because the relationships between concepts are familiar or likely to elicit other associations. For example, the phrases "good boy" and "good zebra" are both formed from familiar words, but the first phrase is more meaningful because the relationship between its parts is more familiar. Other aspects of organization can be involved in meaningfulness, as can be seen by comparing the following organizations of the same list of words:

1. dog, elephant, rabbit, mouse, whale, horse.
2. mouse, rabbit, dog, horse, elephant, whale.

The ordering by size in the second list is more meaningful than the random ordering of the words in the first list because size orderings are familiar.

In studying the ways in which people learn unfamiliar material that lacks meaningfulness, psychologists often invent *nonsense syllables* such as TOV or ZIL to use in their learning experiments. But it is very difficult to invent completely meaningless material; even these nonsense syllables may remind someone of something with which he is already familiar.

In the following discussion *meaningfulness* will be used to refer to the extent to which the material to be learned consists of concepts related to what the student already knows and the extent to which the organization of the material is familiar to him.

HOW CAN THE TEACHER HELP MAKE MATERIAL MEANINGFUL?

It is easier to learn material that has some meaningful relationship than it is to learn material that has a relatively arbitrary relationship. Consider the following string of words:

house, foot, happy, clue, now, rug, sugar, boat, and fat.

That series is much harder to remember than the following one:

the, happy, young, gentleman, placed, the, black, suitcase, in, the, airplane.

The last series of words is more meaningful; it makes sense to the reader. Instead of learning each word by rote, it is possible to remember the thought, the "idea," which organizes the sequence. Or, suppose the task is to learn the letter sequence: OTTFFSSEN-TETTFF. It would be difficult to learn this sequence by rote, but when the learner knows that the sequence consists of the first letters of the words *one, two, three,* etc., to *fifteen,* the task becomes simple. Giving the sequence meaning makes it easy to retain. For a long time educators have known that meaningfulness is an important factor in learning. The important problem here is how the teacher can make use of this principle in the classroom.

Essentially, the teacher's task is to make the material to be learned meaningful to the learner. Material is often meaningful only to the teacher; the learner is at first unable to perceive any theme or structure. We have already seen that people will organize and structure their experiences whenever possible (e.g., the discussion of schemata on page 69). The teacher can aid the student by presenting him with a general schema or plan before dealing with specifics.

When presenting new material, some teachers make the mistake of trying to present isolated facts or elements and then slowly building up to the general structure. What happens is that the students do not remember the material because it is relatively meaningless at the time it is presented. When the student cannot see how one step leads to the next, when he does not know where he is headed, his retention is poor, and he soon becomes lost. Discouraged and frustrated, he may become bored and restless and develop a negative attitude toward the subject. Many people who view arithmetic with distaste probably developed their dislike in just this way. Another danger signal is the students' asking why they should learn particular material. This question often means that the things to be learned are perceived in isolation rather than as part of some structure.

When the teacher observes these warning symptoms, he should not respond with irritation but rather should examine his presentation. Although these symptoms may be the result of other problems, the teacher should first consider lack of structure in the lesson when searching for their cause. Perhaps by switching to a different approach, he might be able to provide the meaningfulness that was lacking. The problem with some subjects—for example, arithmetic—is that it is difficult to present the grand structure in the beginning; one must learn many facts in order for it to make any sense. If a unit of material is meaningless because its structure is too complex, the teacher must offer some structure that does have significance for the learner. The teacher must be sufficiently acquainted with his subject matter and the capabilities of his students to present subparts that have a structure which they can appreciate.

One way to teach a concept is to have the learner "discover" it as the result of an inductive process. First one relation is studied and then another until the student suddenly appreciates (insight?) the existence of the total structure or some general principle. For example, it is possible to have students conduct a number of experiments that illustrate some scientific principle and then have them formulate the principle that is involved. In a science class, students often experiment with weights and levers. By placing one weight a fixed distance from the fulcrum, they can add other weights at various points on the other side and record which combinations result in a balance. Working in small groups, the students attempt to discover the principle involved by formulating and testing various hypotheses. Or, in geography, students might study maps and tabulate the number of major cities situated on a body of water versus other locations. This empirical study can then lead to a discussion of the importance of water in which the students offer hypotheses and consider each other's ideas with a minimum of guidance from the teacher. When such projects are possible, the results are most gratifying to the teacher and exciting to the students. However, there is always the risk that confusion rather than insight will result. With very bright children the dangers are minimized, but caution is still necessary; the teacher should make himself available for guidance and channel the students' work along the right lines.

Once the student has acquired a schema or intellectual structure, he can readily learn compatible material by addition. That is, if something to be learned is meaningful in terms of what has been learned, the student will rapidly assimilate the new material. Actually, meaningfulness is always dependent upon past learning to some extent; indeed the term implies a relationship to the past. Thus the task of making material meaningful is a matter of relating it to what has already been learned by the student, and this is a central task of the teacher. The teacher need not—indeed, should not—be subtle in making such connections. A common error in teaching is the assumption that the connection is obvious to the students, since it is so obvious to the teacher.

The teacher must be in intellectual empathy with his students. He must know what they have already learned before coming to him, and what their major interests are. Without this background the teacher runs the risk of either boring the students with repetitions of earlier experiences or frustrating them by presenting material for which they lack the necessary foundations. One pitfall for the teacher is the tendency to judge a class by extreme members. One bright child sitting in the front row, nodding his head in understanding, is often sufficient to give the inexperienced teacher the impression that the whole class is with him. In a similar way, one slow student who is confused can influence the teacher to gear down the intellectual level of the interaction and repeat explanations, causing most of the class to direct their thoughts and attention elsewhere. If the teacher is aware of individual differences in capacity, he can resolve this problem by presenting students with tasks suitable for their particular capabilities. When the teaching level is too high, the result is high variance in classroom achievement. The brightest students accelerate and the slow are hopelessly lost. Low-level teaching produces low variance in achievement. The slow student learns more than he would otherwise while the bright student learns less.

Since the past experience of the student can be used to make new material meaningful, it is important for the teacher to know something about the social background of the learners. Children of the inner city have had quite different experiences from those of suburban children. These differences are important both in the introduction of new material and the maintenance of interest. For example, in the teaching of reading, the story itself is used to make the task meaningful and interesting. To children from the lowest socioeconomic levels, a story about father coming home in the evening with his brief case and white shirt to an individual house with a two-car garage is usually not a meaningful story. Concern with this problem has recently led to the publication of readers that are realistic in terms of the everyday experiences of children of different social groups. In some second-grade classrooms no child has ever seen a frog or a picture of one and the children are unable to identify one when it is brought for them to observe. "It's a big bug" or "Some kind of lizard" are typical responses. The variety of new experiences the teacher can offer a group like this are very different from what would be needed in many suburban schools.

Another technique for facilitating the transition to new material is the use of familiar terms and phrases when possible. To avoid redundancy, teachers sometimes use different terms or synonyms when introducing new content and thereby weaken the transition for the sake of style. If a synonym for some term is used, the teacher must be sure that the students appreciate that it is a synonym for the concept with which they are already familiar. A meaningful vocabulary is necessary for meaningful teaching. Students must learn new words that are synonymous with previous concepts, but it is the task of the teacher to emphasize the relatedness of the new to the old. "That is right, George; and what other word have we learned that means the same thing?"

In general, the teacher makes material meaningful by clearly explaining it and by relating it to past experiences. In addition to using the past experiences of the students, the teacher provides new realistic experiences. These include, where appropriate, experiments, demonstrations, and discussion of applications. Often the use of models is almost essential to development of understanding. For example, it is usually necessary to use a model when explaining and demonstrating the phases of the moon and the nature of eclipses. When using models, or even verbal analogies, the teacher should realize that to the extent they are not identical to the real phenomena, misconceptions may occur. The usual eclipse model conveys some very misleading impressions about relative sizes and distances, and it usually uses circular orbits when they should be elliptical. The danger with verbal analogies is that students tend to take them in their concrete sense and not appreciate the abstraction. Still waters *do not* run deep. They do not run at all!

WHOLE VS. PART LEARNING

When a student desires to learn certain material, he has two alternative strategies. He can learn the material a part at a time, or he can study the whole selection until he masters it. A poem can be learned by either technique; but which is superior? Several considerations seem to be involved in the answer. If the whole unit has some structure that organizes the parts, it is more efficient to start by studying the whole and then later to study those parts that present special difficulty (provided, of course, that the whole is not unreasonably large). This approach seems to be especially effective for the more intelligent learner. People usually adopt a preferred approach to the memorization of meaningful material, but their preferred technique is often not the technique that should be used for the greatest learning efficiency. Of course, if the material to be learned lacks an overall structure, nothing is gained by using the whole approach, and it may be best to learn the selection a part at a time. The slow learner usually profits from this approach, rather than with the whole method, even when the material is highly structured. For him, the structure itself lacks meaning and thus cannot facilitate learning of the parts. Actually, if this is the case, the student should not be given the task of assimilating the information. He is not ready. He lacks the necessary prerequisites, and to insist that he learn this material will only strengthen his feelings of defeat.

When the material that must be learned is unrelated to previously acquired knowledge, the student must learn it by rote. The dates of historical events, the alphabet, multiplication tables, and capitals of states are some examples. Mnemonic aids can sometimes facilitate learning by introducing an element of meaningfulness with respect to some other context. The teacher should note that arbitrary relations are not only difficult to learn but are soon forgotten. This is true of many dates, formulae, and other isolated facts. A valid curriculum question is whether something meaningful could be substituted for material that is tedious to acquire and unlikely to be retained. It is, however, interesting that we often judge an individual as "well educated" on the basis of his possession of esoteric information that is the result of rote learning. It is more difficult to see real understanding and creative analysis at work. Recognizing the artist or composer from his style is quite a different matter from memorizing many specific titles together with the names of their authors.

LEARNING ABSTRACT CONCEPTS

A special problem arises when the teacher wishes to make an abstract concept meaningful. Abstract concepts become meaningful to the learner to the extent that they are related to experience. Some concepts, however, are easier to relate to definite experiences than are others. Suppose we wish to teach the concept "red" to someone who spoke no English. One approach would be to hold up a red ball and say "red" and then hold up a red sweater and a red toy, again saying "red." The learner would probably appreciate immediately that "red" referred to the quality shared by the objects. If only the ball had been used, the learner might think that "red" referred to its shape or some other quality. Even in this example there is the problem that we may have conveyed the notion that the term refers to a fixed property of objects when actually it is dependent upon conditions of illumination and many other variables.

Many simple sensory abstractions present little difficulty, but suppose the task is to teach the concept "honesty" or "mercy" or "bravery." To make the concept of "honesty" meaningful, the teacher can give examples and can use the term in reference to the student's own behavior. The problem is that the examples seldom illustrate all the shades of meaning of the concept or all the situations in which it is appropriate. The result can be a limited understanding of the concept. When we teach children "honesty," we usually use examples that emphasize honesty toward other individuals. The child learns that it is not honest to take another child's pencil or money. Children are seldom taught honesty in a manner that includes honesty toward institutions or abstract social organizations. As adults, many people will cheat the telephone company or fake an income tax return without feelings of guilt. Yet these same individuals would never dream of cheating another person. The concept of honesty has been learned with a special limited meaning as the result of the manner in which it was taught. Similarly, bravery is often taught and learned as a quality of the hero. Bravery in everyday life is a foreign concept to many people. Mercy becomes associated with the nurse and as a result takes on special connotations.

From these examples we can see that the maturity of the students and the nature of their prior experiences are critical in relating abstract concepts to past experience. Valid examples of honesty or bravery will also differ from one social class to another. One weakness of the honor system used by many colleges is the requirement that one report a peer if he is seen cheating. Children are taught in their early years that they should not "tattle" or carry tales; then suddenly they are told that the reverse is the honorable action. To many of them, this is an alien and unacceptable meaning of honor; it conflicts with past experience.

In teaching many concepts, the teacher cannot give every possible example, but he should try to consider whether or not he is presenting the major instances of its use. If the teacher is aware of this problem, he can at least avoid giving only illustrations which represent some limited usage.

THE TRANSFER OF LEARNING

How does the teacher know when his teaching has been meaningful? Usually class discussion of a problem requiring application of what has been learned quickly reveals the quality of the learning. William James gives an example of class discussion that clearly reveals the absence of meaningful learning:

> A friend of mine, visiting a school, was asked to examine a young class in geography. Glancing at the book she said: "Suppose you should dig a hole in the ground, hundreds of feet deep, how should you find it at the bottom—warmer or cooler than on top?" None of the class replying, the teacher said, "I am sure they know, but I think you don't ask the question quite rightly. Let me try." So taking the book she asked: "In what condition is the interior of the globe?" and received the immediate answer from half the class at once: "The interior of the globe is in a condition of igneous fusion."[1]

There are many examples of students' learning by rote material the teacher thought meaningful. The misquotes of pledges, songs, and other material by children are often quite amusing but at the same time disturbing to the educator because of their implications. The child has merely complied with the teacher's mandate that the selection must be learned. Not only does the task lack meaning for the child, but, perhaps more seriously, the teacher is cast into the role of one who requires uninteresting and tedious tasks. When the student can *transfer* what he has learned to the understanding of some related material or to the solution of a new problem, the teacher knows that what the student learned has meaning for him.

All education is based on a very important assumption—that what is learned in the classroom may be employed in other situations, or, in other terms, that changes in behavior acquired in the classroom are not confined to the classroom. The term *transfer* is used to designate the manifestation of learning in a situation different from the situation in which the learning took place. If we denied the existence of transfer, it would be tantamount to saying that one learns in school in order to do better in school. When we are talking about the acquisition of basic skills, we might say that one does learn in school in order to do better in school, but perhaps it would be more accurate to say that in such a case some things are learned as a prerequisite to further learning. However, the ultimate goal of schooling is to equip the individual with a set of skills and certain knowledge that will allow him to function successfully in the adult society outside of the classroom.

It is obvious that transfer does in fact take place. The person who learned to read in elementary school using special textbooks is able, as an adult, to read anything from his evening paper to advertisements written with smoke in the sky. Again, having learned to count in school using a relatively limited range of objects, the adult is able to count the members of any class of objects. Transfer occurs at every level of the education enterprise; in his private practice the new physician uses techniques that he acquired in medical school, just as the engineer computes stresses and loads using principles that he learned in college. Knowing that transfer of school learning does occur still leaves several important questions. Under what conditions does transfer occur? Is transfer always beneficial? How can the teacher promote the transfer of what is learned in the classroom?

WHEN DOES TRANSFER OCCUR?

Typically, transfer occurs when a new situation has certain similarities to a situation in which learning has already taken place. Thorndike used the concept of *identical elements* to explain the phenomenon. According to this concept, if a new situation has stimulus elements similar to an old situation, those responses that had been learned to those stimulus elements in the original situation will occur in the new situation. The "response" that is transferred may be a specific act, a method of approach to a problem, or a principle which can be applied.

Pavlov would have employed a similar explanation. Any situation consists of an array of stimulus elements—$S_1, S_2, S_3, S_4, S_5, S_6$. If an organism learns to make certain responses in the situation, those responses are connected with each of the stimulus elements. At a later time, a subset of the original stimulus array, e.g., S_2 and S_5, may elicit the responses that were learned to the total array. A person putting together a jigsaw puzzle usually recognizes what it is going to be long before he has all of the elements in place. The elements, or parts, that he sees are sufficient to elicit the response that was learned in connection with the total configuration. Or, a child at the zoo will recognize that a strange animal is, indeed, an animal because of the stimulus elements it has in common with other things he calls "animals." This occurs even though the strange animal, for example, a kangaroo, may lack some of the elements conspicuous in creatures more familiar to him and may also have unique characteristics of its own.

The feeling of familiarity that one has when in a neighborhood drugstore is a response to many stimulus elements—the location of the counter and the magazine stand, the elderly pharmacist, and other details. In a strange city, a person may walk into a drugstore and have "the strange feeling that I have been here before." This uncanny sensation is known as *déjà vu*, "already seen." The feeling of familiarity has been aroused because the second situation contained several of the same elements possessed by the drugstore back home. If the two situations were almost identical, the person might consciously recognize the similarity, but it is possible to have the feeling of having been there before without knowing why it looks familiar. However, our basic concern is with the empirical nature of transfer rather than with theoretical explanation.

POSITIVE AND NEGATIVE TRANSFER

Transfer may be either positive or negative, depending upon whether performance is facilitated or interfered with as a result of prior learning. Consider two equivalent groups. One group has learning experience A and another group does not. Later, both groups are called upon to perform in situation B. If the group that had learning experience A performs better on task B than the group that did not have A, there has been positive transfer. But if the group that did not have A does better on B, then there has been negative transfer from A to B.

In some cases, however, there may be no transfer at all—either positive or negative. In one study it was found that when

	Previous Learning Experience	**New Situation**
Group I	A	B
Group II	Not A	B

high school graduates were asked to explain the phases of the moon, there was negative transfer from what they had learned about the nature of eclipses.[2] The majority of the students stated that the phases of the moon were caused by the shadow of the earth. Similarly, the emphasis on the importance of oxygen led many students to state that it was the most prevalent gas in the air. In contrast, almost every student could name the two common temperature scales. Even though this represents rote learning, there seems to be no competing responses and no negative transfer.

When the teacher knows that certain concepts are subject to negative transfer, he should take special care to reduce the probable confusion when teaching these concepts. The confusion between the eclipse and the phases of the moon could be reduced by more emphasis on their differences. People who are in doubt about the distinction are readily convinced when shown that it is possible to see a phase moon in the daytime where any possible effect of the earth's shadow is logically ruled out. The teacher who does not know that this is a likely area of confusion will fail to make the critical distinctions. The specific mistakes made by learners are important data for the teacher. When many students make the same mistake, the problem is often negative transfer. If there is no pattern to the errors, then it is likely that there was general confusion rather than a specific misunderstanding. Positive or negative transfer also occurs from learning task to learning task and can occur both forwards and backwards. Suppose two equivalent groups both learn A and then one of the groups learns B. If we retest the two groups on A, we may find a difference. Should the group that learned B do better or worse than the other group on the re-test of A, then we conclude that the learning of B had a *retroactive* effect on the retention of A. One can readily see that if a list of dates is memorized, the memorization of a second list will reduce the accuracy with which the first list can be recalled, while if a list of names is memorized, the learning of a story using these names will facilitate recall of the original list. In education the concern is usually with *proactive* positive transfer. Proactive positive transfer occurs when an individual who has learned A can learn B more readily than someone who has not learned A.

The whole concept of the curriculum is based on two essential elements. First, certain material should be learned and certain skills acquired—the value system determines the choice of what should be learned. Second, some forms of learning must take place before other forms can be acquired. This ordering of subject matter attempts to maximize proactive positive transfer. Part of the concept of *readiness* is the fact that a person must learn certain things before he can learn specific additional material or that he must develop particular skills before he can develop others. Not all learning that takes place in the classroom is important because it can be transferred outside of the school. Some learning is important only because it permits other learning which is valued; this is the major importance of learning to read. There are, then, two reasons for teaching—either what is taught is valued or what is taught permits the learning of something valued.

In general, positive transfer occurs when two situations are similar and the appropriate responses are the same. For example, if a student learns to solve certain physics problems involving levers and weights, he should have no trouble solving similar problems even though the size of the weights or the length of the lever or other details have been changed. If the student does have difficulties, it may be that he cannot transfer a meaningful principle because he failed to learn it in the first place and instead memorized some specific case. Chemistry and physics are two disciplines in which students often fail because they rely on rote learning without understanding the principles. There are ways to avoid this predilection of some students. One way is to minimize the value of rote memorization. In a chemistry or physics test the teacher can provide the equations and thus emphasize knowing applications rather than details. When students know that a test will be an "open book" exam, they are much less likely to memorize details and are more apt to concentrate on important relationships and applications. After all, if one knows how to apply an equation, he can always find it when necessary.

The transfer of motor skills is an important part of everyday life. A prime example is the ease with which a person can quickly adjust to driving different cars. Even though a new car "feels strange," the quality of the driver's performance reveals high positive transfer.

Negative transfer is strongest when new responses must be made in situations very like ones in which other responses have already been learned. Imagine what would happen if it were decided that henceforth cars will go on the red light and stop on the green. Even if all drivers agreed to the change, past habits would produce disastrous results. If, instead, orange were substituted for the red and blue for the green, there would be considerable positive transfer. Most students would agree that holding a very heavy weight is certainly hard work. Yet "work" as a concept in physics requires that the weight be in motion against an opposing force. Because of negative transfer from the popular concept, students have difficulty with the technical use of the term.

It is obvious, to answer one of our original questions, that transfer is not always beneficial. When a person must make new responses to old stimuli, the old responses that were originally learned to the stimuli tend to intrude, and the result is negative transfer. Positive transfer occurs when old responses can be used in responding to new stimuli. There is no source of interference, and the previously developed skill in making the response is an asset. Most situations contain elements of both positive and negative transfer. When the child shifts from printing to cursive writing, there is positive transfer of dexterity, spelling, and punctuation skills, but negative transfer from the tendency to print a letter when it should be written. Spontaneous transfer, both positive and negative, is likely to occur to the extent that the new stimuli are similar to the old stimuli. Whether the transfer is positive or negative is determined by whether or not the learned behavior is appropriate in the new situation.

HOW CAN THE TEACHER PROMOTE TRANSFER?

At one time, the question of the teacher's role in promoting transfer would not have been raised. The assumption of "formal discipline" was that transfer automatically took place from specific subjects to life outside the school. The rigorous study of geometry and formal logic was believed to make one rigorous and logical in thinking regardless of the problem under consideration. Memorization of Greek and Latin was considered "mental discipline." The mind was supposed to be exercised, like a muscle, and as a result made quick and powerful.

A vast wealth of research failed to support the basic tenets of formal discipline. Among those studies were the now classical investigations which showed that the learning of Latin had relatively little effect upon performance in English unless the transition was emphasized. Similar investigations found that the study of geometry had little effect upon the rigor of one's general thinking. The important principle which has emerged from such research is that transfer is promoted when the teacher teaches for transfer; there is little transfer if it is erroneously assumed that there will be adequate spontaneous transfer, especially when the relationships are subtle. Students must be motivated to transfer what they have learned, and practice in transfer to new situations must be part of most classroom lessons. Practice in generalizing relationships to new situations is the essence of training for transfer. After a class in ecology has studied the ways in which the teeth and digestive systems of animals are adapted to their feeding habits, the class can be given the task of discovering the many other forms of adaptation to the environment that are represented in various species. The teacher should supply the minimum amount of guidance that will guarantee adequate transfer. At times the transfer can be made quite direct. After discussion of heat expansion and demonstrations of the phenomenon, the teacher might ask, "Why do you think that spaces are left between the blocks of concrete when a sidewalk is poured?" Most students will accomplish the transfer without difficulty, and they will learn a practical application at the same time. Or, the learning of a Latin root can lead to an attempt to discover as many English words as possible that are derived from Latin. Sometimes specific elements are transferred; at other times general principles. While the latter is more appealing since it suggests understanding and meaningfulness, both aspects of transfer are important. It is very useful to know that 5 x 7 equals 35 as a rote fact, for it would be tedious to get the answer by the use of a general principle each time.

The most effective way to learn how to perform in a situation is to learn in that situation—i.e., "learning by doing," a fundamental aspect of John Dewey's reaction to formal discipline. "On-the-job training" is a familiar part of our culture, but it is not really new. Apprenticeship is a very old and very effective way of learning. If one lives on a farm, one learns quite a lot about farming, or if one works for a printer, one learns most of the important aspects of that trade.

While it may seem obvious that learning in a situation is more effective than learning material designed for transfer to that situation, there are subtle aspects to consider. No matter how cautious we are in designing a curriculum, the real-life situation will contain components which we have overlooked. These might include special skills or even involve personality considerations that evade any formal analysis to abstract the essentials. Since the values of modern education do not demand early selection of a trade or profession, there is a commitment to a general education. A good general education keeps many doors open; that is, it maximizes the variety of career paths open to the individual. It is dangerous to determine the occupational possibilities for an individual before his interests have matured. The schools serve to offset the predilection of many parents to press their children into careers for the wrong reasons. The fact that Dad is a physician or the chance gift of a chemistry set can produce results that everyone later regrets. The enthusiasms of youth are often just that.

Even though the values of education prevent immersing the individual in real roles for a prolonged time, there are worth-while approximations to reality. It is possible to promote transfer to situations outside the classroom through the use of *simulations* of specific situations. Many degrees of realism are possible. Consider the following two problems that might be given to a student in the third grade: How much is 4 times 9? If one pencil costs 4 cents, how much will it cost to buy 9 pencils? In both problems the arithmetic is the same, but the latter uses a practical context. The student realizes that the skill to be learned has some relevance for him and is not merely a whim of the teacher; the task is meaningful. A simulation of a store with buyers and sellers can make the worth of arithmetic skills even more obvious. To the extent that the simulation is successful, the learner acquires all of the skills he needs for the real situation. More detailed discussion of simulations as a teaching technique will be presented in Chapter Six.

The teacher must teach his students to expect a relationship between what they are learning and general application of this learning to other situations. This may seem obvious and simple to many who have not yet taught, but the implications will disturb those who fear being challenged by the learners in their charge. If students learn to seek relationships, they will demand to know why they are learning what they are when the relevance seems obscure. When a student asks "Why do we need to know that?" the teacher should be both pleased and concerned—pleased because the student has learned to seek transfer, to search for the larger relationships, but at the same time concerned that what he offered seemed to lack meaningfulness. The lazy teacher who is not committed to the values of education will be content with a passive, if bored, audience that does not make "trouble" and does not "interrupt" the prepared "lesson for today." This may seem the easy way, but it is small wonder that these teachers soon come to dislike their profession. It is no more interesting to them than it is to the students.

The most gratifying experience to the teacher is seeing students come to seek transfer without specific prompting. In one eighth-grade earth science class the discussion of air included its role in communication—carrying the vibrations that permit speech and hearing. After a moment's reflection, one student excitedly announced that people would not be able to speak to each other on the moon because of the absence of air. This transfer took place because three components were present—past information (the moon has no air), the understanding of a new principle (air is required for sound propagation), and motivation to seek transference. At other times, appropriate prompting leads to the mental leap. In a tenth-grade biology class the teacher asked about the curious fact that the cactus is covered with thorns. One boy quickly responded, "They have thorns so that they will not be eaten." The student was prompted with the question, "How do you suppose the cactus knows that if it grows thorns it will not be eaten?" Everyone was amused, but the point was made, and the student said, "I guess I should have said that the cactus does not get eaten because it has thorns." The teleological error was corrected when the student perceived that he could not freely transfer the concept of volition. The difference between this form of teacher-learner interaction and rote drill can be the difference between excitement and drudgery.

Some very misguided teachers give additional homework as a punishment, or have students write words, or do arithmetic problems after school. These teachers never seem to realize that through this reprehensible practice they are conceding that these activities are unpleasant, that they are, in fact, punishment. It would not be surprising to find that teachers who give extra drill as punishment are the same teachers who depend upon drill as a teaching technique. Sometimes drill may be useful or even necessary, but it should not be preferred over other techniques that accomplish the same objectives.

The more intelligent the student, the more successful he will be in transferring what is learned in one situation to related situations. The less able student has more difficulty with transfer and is easily frustrated in his efforts. Some transfer, however, requires less ability than others. Transfer to a very similar situation can be achieved by almost all individuals, while transfer to remotely or abstractly related situations may be too demanding for most. The teacher has an obligation to assess the capacity of each student. Through the use of graded tasks, individual students can be challenged to reach goals that are within their reach. In this way, students with quite different abilities can still know the gratification of success and be spared either excessive frustration or boredom. It should not be necessary for the teacher to have to choose between frustrating some students and boring others.

There is no one correct technique for providing practice on the transfer of learning. In fact, the use of only one technique would be limited and boring.

In summary, the teacher can do a number of things to increase the likelihood that his students will transfer what they have learned to situations that differ from the specific context in which the learning took place. The teacher can teach for transfer by pointing out examples of how the material under consideration has other applications. In a Latin class that has just learned that *sub* means "under," the teacher could point out the relation to words the students know—*submarine*, *subway*, or *submerge*. Or, after a discussion of factors that affect the freezing point of water, the teacher could point out the application of these principles in the use of antifreeze. Students can be asked to produce applications or similar examples as practice in looking for transfer possibilities.

"We have seen that the turtle's shell protects him from enemies. What other animals can you think of that use this defense?" Or, "What are some other ways that animals protect themselves from danger?"

When this approach is frequently used, the students not only receive practice in transfer but come to *expect* that this is what is wanted. Once the learner develops the attitude that what is learned has meaning outside of a limited context, he will begin to search for relationships on his own initiative. When this does not happen, teachers are heard to say of their charges, "I have a bright class. They have no trouble learning, but I can't get them to *think*." When this happens, it would be worth while for the teacher to reflect upon whether he has been placing a premium upon rote memory of facts and principles rather than upon their imaginative use in new situations. Simulations and other devices provide practice in transfer, but what is really critical is the development of attitudes or habits of thought that make transfer an active rather than passive process.

CAN CREATIVITY BE TAUGHT?

Educators often state that they want to teach their students to be creative. Whether this is possible is a complex question. Part of this complexity results from the problem of just what is meant by *creativity*. When pressed for an explanation of exactly what it is that they want of their students, the replies are usually very general and rather vague. Originality is usually mentioned, and there also tends to be the implication that the production should be of high quality. Thus quality enters the definition of creativity as an educational value, for the dictionary defines creativity only in terms of "bringing into existence" and "newness."

Creativity and originality seem to be related, and arguments about the two concepts can usually be resolved by semantic analysis; that is, the definition of creativity chosen determines the role of originality. Creativity in art and creativity in problem solving differ in the objectivity of the criterion. A creative solution to a problem can be operationally defined as a solution that works, i.e., solves the problem, and that does not occur to most individuals. Important inventions such as the airplane or the paper clip would be examples. Also included here would be the more abstract insights that have valuable applications. For a work of art to be considered creative, it must be approved by certain groups who are considered capable of judging its worth. The term *creative* is of course used in more general ways. Talking about a class of thirty-five first-graders, a teacher will explain, "Finger-painting gives all of them a chance to do something creative." It is obvious that there is no general agreement on how the term should be used.

THE RELATIONSHIP BETWEEN CREATIVITY AND TRANSFER

The creative problem solver is often the one who is able to see that a new situation is similar to one with which he has had experience and thus can transfer what he knows. A less able individual may have had the same earlier experiences but be unable to perceive the similarities between the new and the old. Every great scientist had contemporaries who had access to the same facts but were unable to transfer them to the critical problem. An examination of the great insights in the history of ideas would reveal that certain gifted individuals had successfully brought pre-existing knowledge to bear in the solution of their problem. Often others had the necessary data but lacked the ability to bridge the gap because the transfer was not obvious. According to the legend, Archimedes did not solve the problem of specific gravity in isolation from other information. He was said to have transferred the data he acquired seeing his own body displace water to the solution of the new problem. People who successfully solve new problems, i.e., who are creative, first acquire all of the available data that seems relevant. This strategy maximizes the likelihood of transfer. Occasionally the existing data and concepts are misleading; they create a mental set that prevents thinking in new ways. This accounts for the success of the tyro who is not so burdened. But these cases are relatively rare.

ENCOURAGING CREATIVITY

To the extent that creativity depends upon transfer, the answer to whether it can be taught seems to be that students can be taught thinking habits which will allow them to be creative. It is probably much easier to develop these habits of thought in the first years of school than to attempt later to change ways of thinking that have become firmly set as the result of constricted experience. The child who comes from a home where fantasy is not frowned upon may well have a permanent advantage over the child who has had five years of discipline in thinking along highly restricted lines. Research has shown that creative individuals spend more time daydreaming than do less creative individuals. Naturally, too much daydreaming can be pathological if it becomes a substitute for effort and achievement, but there seems to be an optimum between the two extremes.

The role of any one experience in the home is difficult to evaluate because of the correlation between the presence of one activity and the presence of others. In the home that permits fantasy, there will probably be more reading of stories to children, more educational toys, and more excursions to museums. In the homes where fantasy is discouraged, there will probably be few books, the adults will spend as little time as possible talking with their children, and "Don't bother me with so many questions" will often be heard. In general, some homes place greater value on intellectual activities and the broadening of the child's horizon of experience than others. To some extent, these homes teach children to expect transfer, to search for relations between past experiences and new situations. We have seen that the teacher can develop these expectancies. In some cases the home has made the teacher's job easier, while in others the child's early environment places the teacher under a handicap.

A major obstacle to creativity is the tendency to persevere in old ways of handling problems, even though they may no longer be successful. Learned ways of behaving and thinking are called *response sets*. Often it is necessary to "break" a set in order to cope with a new problem. By way of illustration, in one study a group was given several objects, including a box of thumbtacks and a candle, and was told to fasten the candle in an upright position on the side of a door. The problem proved to be quite difficult. When the same materials were given to another group, but with the thumbtacks outside of the thumbtack box, the problem was quickly solved. The second group used the thumbtacks to tack the thumbtack box to the door and then set the candle in it. The first group was inhibited by a "set"; because the tacks were in the box, they thought of the box as a container for the tacks. Once they thought of the box as a container, it was very difficult to see it in a new way. The second group was not inhibited since the materials were presented in a manner which avoided the set.[3]

The response set which interfered with the solution to this problem can be viewed as an example of negative transfer. People have learned to respond to the container in a particular manner. The task requires that new responses be made to the old stimulus, and this is usually difficult. The old responses tend to occur, but they are no longer appropriate. In the present illustration, old and new responses refers to old and new ways of thinking about the objects used in the task. *Functional fixedness* is the term often used to describe the difficulty people have when they must disregard the usual function of an object and discover a new way in which it can be used.

Children can be taught to throw off sets and think of the world around them in new ways. They can be encouraged to use their imagination, and they can be rewarded for their efforts. "Let us see how many things we can think of that are round" or "How many different ways could you use a stone?" The teacher can start with some examples that encourage the children to seek wide variety. "Well, we could use a little stone as a weight on a fishing line, and we could use a big stone like a hammer to drive a stake." If the teacher lists the responses on the board, the children are highly motivated to think of as many responses as possible. By giving approval to rather far-fetched contributions, the teacher rewards thinking which is not conventional. This approach can be combined with almost any subject matter. "In how many different ways is the force of gravity important to man?" "What are some of the ways in which our city could be made into a better place to live?" "How many objects can we think of that contain a right angle (or circles, parallel lines, etc.)?" "Let us see how many words we can find that have the sound 'ā,' as in *fate*."

The rigid teacher often penalizes creative thinking by rejecting responses that differ from what he is seeking. Even though some specific response is being sought, the teacher who wishes to encourage creative thinking will reward novel contributions. If a student gives an answer that shows he has been thinking, he should be rewarded, not given the impression that he was completely wrong. Too often, we hear a teacher say "No, that is not right. Someone else?" It would be far better for the teacher to say, "That is very interesting. Tell us, Sally, why you chose that answer." Sally's response may show considerable insight and may bring out points worthy of further discussion by the class. The poor teacher has the set that there is one right answer, and the class soon comes to accept this as the rule. This tendency of the inadequate teacher may often stem from his insecurity rather than from any lack of knowledge.

Even in the teaching of art, where we would expect freedom from constraint, we find practices that constrict rather than broaden the creativity of the learner. Sometimes children are told not to outline their drawings, but Leger and others follow this practice, and their work hangs in museums. Or, children are told that their drawing of the tree does not look like a tree, as if this is a fault that should be corrected. The teacher of art who wishes to preserve the creative feeling will support the child by seeing the merit of his production. By viewing the productions of other children and of artists, the child learns that his approach is one of many.

It may well be that the teacher does not teach his students to be creative but, rather, *allows* them to be creative. Relatively little is known about the factors that produce a creative individual, including the relative importance of heredity and environment. The teacher who encourages imagination and variety, who builds his students' self-confidence in their own productions and who encourages transfer will not need to worry about "teaching" children to be creative. What the teacher values in the classroom is a major determinant of what he finally achieves. The teacher who is creative will induce these values in students even when he is not consciously directing attention to that goal.

THE TRANSFER OF ATTITUDES

The transfer of learned content is important, but the transfer of other forms of learning is also critical. There is a double relation between transfer and attitudes. Certain attitudes are important in obtaining transfer in general, and attitudes are themselves subject to transfer from situation to situation. We have seen that the attitude of self-confidence and the attitude that what is learned in the classroom has significance elsewhere are essential in promoting transfer. The attitude that new ways of doing and perceiving are valued also contributes its share.

What are some of the other attitudes that should be developed in the classroom? Naturally the word *should* reflects a value system, but it also assumes that the attitudes in question *can* be learned and transferred. Taking the definition of teaching as "causing to learn," the teacher can and should teach attitudes. Or, to take a more fundamental stand, the teacher cannot avoid teaching attitudes. Typically, attitudes are learned as a by-product of some classroom activity; one does not usually set out to learn an attitude. This is not to say that the teacher does not intend that particular attitudes be learned, but the teaching of attitudes is sometimes an exception to the rule that for the most efficient learning, the learner should know what it is that he should learn.

GENERAL ATTITUDES TOWARD EDUCATION

One of the most important attitudes that is learned in the early years of school is the attitude toward the school situation and the basic activity of learning, but failures in this realm are very pervasive. A considerable number of students say they do not like school, and they avoid it at every opportunity. The large number of high school dropouts is a dramatic and widely publicized facet of the problem.

Why are negative attitudes toward school so prevalent? It seems to be that, for many students, unpleasant experiences in the classroom outweigh positive, pleasant experiences. In addition, if activities outside the school are more enjoyable and satisfying, there is a very one-sided competition for the students' attention. It is interesting to note that when a child is detained after school as punishment, there is the explicit implication that it is better to be elsewhere than in school. In fact, many teachers do not keep students after school because they feel it is punishment for themselves as well.

The unpleasant experiences that produce negative attitudes toward school are of several varieties. For too many people, school is a failure experience that continually threatens their self-esteem. Often a vicious circle develops in which an individual's failures lead to decreased interest and motivation, which in turn lead to further failures. A cumulative aversion to the school environment develops unless the circle is broken. Since much school learning is contingent upon having learned other material earlier, the student who has not profited from past school experience has a double disadvantage—negative attitudes and lack of readiness for the new learning tasks that confront him. Empirical studies of classroom achievement show that the discrepancy between high-achievers and under-achievers is greater in fourth grade than it was in the first grade, and the discrepancy becomes still greater later on. If there were a constant difference over the years, we might be tempted to emphasize differences existing before the beginning of school and place less emphasis on the school experience. However, the most plausible view seems to be that there is a cumulative interaction between the school experience and individual differences in ability, attitudes, and motivation.

When the teacher insures that the school experience provides each learner with positive rewards that outweigh the negative, the learner will form desirable attitudes that will transfer to future learning situations. He will come to *expect* success in the classroom. The teacher can achieve this end by setting tasks for each learner that are within his reach. Through the use of graded tasks, each learner can know the pleasure of success and the resultant feeling of increased self-esteem. Care must be taken to avoid the indiscriminate use of "easy" tasks in the classroom, for that practice has several hidden faults. One fault is that if all tasks are undemanding, there is no challenge. If there is no challenge, there is no feeling of success in achievement; in fact, boredom will be the result. It is desirable for the learner to feel that it is *likely* that he will be correct in his performance, but he should not feel that success is always guaranteed. People soon lose interest in a game that they always win. This principle is less true of very young children, but it develops quickly as the child grows older. Boredom can create negative attitudes toward school as certainly as constant failure. Both situations are to be avoided.

The teacher who wishes to avoid both frustration and boredom is faced with several basic problems. The typical classroom is large, and the students are not a homogeneous group with respect to the important variables for learning—motivation, abilities, and attitudes. It is not simple to evaluate each student's ability and inclination to learn. Knowledge of a student's performance is not enough, as a highly motivated student of average ability may perform at the same level as a student of high ability with reduced motivation. Normally the teacher has information from standardized ability tests to use as part of the evaluation of each student's performance. From a student's participation in the classroom and his written work, the teacher can decide whether the student is having too many failure experiences or if he is not receiving sufficient challenge.

Sometimes the students can be grouped into relatively homogeneous groups—a prevalent practice in the teaching of reading. Each group receives a reasonable challenge, and the challenge can be maintained by changing the group membership when warranted. When subgroups are not used, graded tasks are still possible. The teacher can address to the entire class a question that can be handled by all members and then call on one of the least advanced students. Similarly, other material used will challenge the most advanced. It is possible to reward different levels of sophistication even though the problem is the same. For example, in a discussion of why we need to pay taxes, students of both high and low ability should be rewarded for their efforts even though the quality of their production differs.

Even a wrong answer need not mean complete failure. By asking further questions or giving more information, the teacher can often guide the student to a point where he realizes his response was wrong and corrects it himself. This is one of the most gratifying experiences, both to the student and to the teacher. Instead of being a source of punishment, the teacher has, in effect, been of assistance in an event where the student's satisfaction rewards him for his own efforts. This is very important because outside of the classroom there is no teacher to say "good" or "that is right." The ability to receive reward from satisfaction with one's own efforts is essential for the maintenance of learning activities later in life. At the same time the student develops a positive self-evaluation which includes confidence in the ability to achieve. These attitudes are much more important to an individual in the pursuit of a successful career and a happy life than much of the specific content learning that occurs in the early school years.

Another problem for many teachers is coping with negative attitudes toward education that some students have developed in previous classrooms or at home. Negative attitudes transfer as well as positive attitudes, and they often make the teacher's task far more difficult than it is when the students have positive or even neutral attitudes. The ways to eliminate negative attitudes are essentially the same as the previously discussed techniques for promoting positive attitudes. The road is a steeper one, for the teacher must reverse the student's perception of the school and alter his expectations about the results of his efforts. Obviously, the more long-standing the history of defeat, the greater will be the student's resistance to change. It is quite a different matter to attempt to change attitudes toward education once the student has reached the high school years than it is to induce changes in the second or third grade. In some cases even the best of teachers may be unable to bring about a basic change in attitudes toward the school, especially when there is so little time to devote to any one individual. If ever the worn cliché about an ounce of prevention being worth a pound of cure is true, it is true of the development of desirable attitudes toward the school, the teacher, and the learning experience.

Not all of the important attitudes in the teaching-learning process are learned in the classroom. Attitudes in the home toward education and intellectual activities exert a strong influence. The attitudes of significant figures, for example, the father of the young boy, can operate to support or defeat the school. The self-concept which has been formed in the preschool years is transferred to the classroom. Normally the child entering school has a very high evaluation of himself. He thinks he is bright, strong, and attractive, and he believes that he will do well in school. He has this self-concept because it was reinforced in the home, primarily by his parents. When children perceive themselves in this way, the school has an initial advantage in its task—an advantage which it should not lose. Unfortunately, some children start school without this advantage. Children who have been made to feel inadequate at home transfer this perception into the classroom. They do not expect to do well, and if the teacher fails to intervene, this becomes a self-fulfilling prophecy.

ATTITUDES TOWARD SPECIFIC EDUCATIONAL EXPERIENCES

Most people form attitudes toward specific aspects of their school experience in addition to a general attitude toward education. These specific attitudes transfer to different situations later in life.

We have all heard people state, "I don't like math" or "History is boring." These specific attitudes can influence future decisions about taking courses and about pursuing a particular career. For example, college students often ask their advisor, "What can I pick as a major that does not require mathematics?" The teacher of a particular subject causes students to learn attitudes toward that subject, and toward education in general, as a simultaneous by-product of his presentation. It may well be more difficult to develop positive attitudes toward some subjects than others, but the teacher of these subjects should rise to the challenge rather than accept the situation as unalterable. It should come as no surprise that the courses people say they liked most in school are usually those in which they received the highest grades. They also identify these same courses as the ones that were taught better than subjects that they liked less.

Attitudes developed toward volunteering and speaking in front of others in the classroom can be transferred to the future years of education and to the social and occupational environments of daily life. The tendency either to be acquiescent or to stand up for one's convictions may receive differential reinforcement in the classroom. Attitudes toward authority are one of the critical consequences of teacher-student interaction. These are only a few of the traits, which we call "personality," that are modified by the school experience. Some traits are encouraged, while others receive no reinforcement or are actively discouraged.

The school is an important agency in the socialization of the individual, and many social attitudes developed there will be transferred to the continually expanding world of the learner. A person develops his social expectations and his style of social behavior through interaction with others. A significant proportion of this interaction occurs in the classroom. One learns about the needs of others and comes to realize that successful social encounters require that the others receive some gratification. The child learns that it is not in his self-interest to be too selfish, and he begins to develop empathy. He learns the value of understanding the other person's point of view. Differential reinforcement brings about an elaborate system of social expectations. He learns to expect to be liked or disliked, to be chosen by others or to expect rejection. In effect, the child develops subjective probabilities connected to the outcome of various social relations.

It is possible for the teacher to identify those children who are social isolates and aid them in becoming more effective members of the class. One frequently used sociometric technique is based on the social choices of the group. The children are asked to list the names of the other members of the class that they would like to

FIGURE IV.1. *A Sample Sociogram Showing Friendship Choices of Five Children*

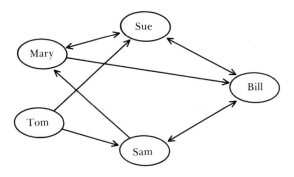

invite to a party or to have on their team. The results can be plotted in a pattern which is called a *sociogram.* In the illustration above the arrow from Mary to Sue indicates that Mary chose Sue. The double arrow between Bill and Sam shows that they chose each other; that is, their choices were reciprocated. The popularity of Sue and Bill and the social isolation of Tom are clearly revealed by the pattern of choices. Tom may be well on the way toward the development of negative social attitudes and pessimistic social expectations. The teacher can intervene by attempting to involve Tom in more group activities and trying to determine the severity and source of the difficulty. Only then will Tom develop satisfactory social attitudes that can be transferred to future social encounters, both in the classroom and elsewhere.

•

CHAPTER FIVE

Motivation

in the

Classroom

•

What is meant by *motivation*? Teachers tell parents, "Sally is bright enough to do the work, but she lacks sufficient motivation." The college freshman complains that he is not motivated to spend more time on his studies. Both the person using the concept of motivation and his audience seem to understand what is meant by the term and act as though they agree on the meaning. However, we cannot assume that the meaning really is always clear. For our present purposes, it is necessary to examine the ways in which the concept is used, and its relation to similar concepts, and then to accept a working definition that will permit detailed consideration of the role of motivation in the teaching-learning process. There are many theories of motivation, but our primary concern is with what occurs in the classroom. Therefore, we will not consider some special facets of motivation and subtle aspects of theory.

Motivation is usually used in reference to some directed activity; a person is motivated *to* (work, study, or read). The purposive nature of behavior is emphasized whenever motivation is discussed. The etiology of the term *motivation* goes back to the Latin verb *movere*—"to move." When a person is motivated to reach a goal, his activity consists of movement toward that goal. The term *drive* has many similar connotations, to both the layman and the scientist. Psychologists study the hunger drive or thirst drive in organisms that have been deprived of food and water. A man who has missed a meal may be quite hungry—i.e., his hunger drive is high—but he will not usually seek food in general. Instead, he will form a specific intention, to buy a good steak or perhaps to make himself a ham sandwich. The point we wish to emphasize is that with people and the higher animals, the primary physiological drives (e.g., hunger, thirst, and sex) produce goal-oriented behavior, but the specific form of the goal and the manner of approach is determined by complex learning. The hungry man never needed to learn to be hungry, but he did have to learn to desire a steak. In other cultures, an equally hungry man would orient his behavior toward obtaining rice or perhaps toward catching a fish.

The physiological drives, which are not learned, are called *primary needs*. The learned needs are known as *secondary needs*. Learned social needs are an example of the many secondary needs that direct human behavior. The need for approval, the need to be with others, and the need to have influence over others are specific social needs. Both primary and secondary needs motivate people to behave in a manner that will allow them to gain goals which will satisfy these needs. For our purpose of discussing motivation in the classroom, we will say that an individual is motivated when he reveals by words or actions that he desires to reach some goal. To motivate an individual is to increase his need to reach some goal or to create a need where there was none. The goal is the *incentive* for motivated behavior, and the specific need is the *motive* for this behavior.

THE MEASUREMENT OF MOTIVATION

If a teacher has a student who does very well in algebra and another who does poorly, the teacher cannot assume that these two students differ in their motivation to learn. One obvious possibility is that even though they both have the same desire to learn, one has a greater intellectual capacity. Achievement is, then, a measure of motivation only when we have sufficient information about the individual's capacity for achievement. Almost every experienced teacher at one time or another, has had occasion to say, "It is not that Tom is not bright. He just does not try!" This statement is based on the teacher's decision that there is, in fact, a discrepancy between what Tom accomplishes and what he is capable of accomplishing. How does the teacher know that Tom is not exerting the effort that he might? There are several possible sources of this information, but they are not all equally reliable.

It may be that Tom has as high a score on intelligence tests as other students who are performing at a superior level. Information obtained from standardized intelligence and aptitude tests are often used to estimate capacity for achievement in the classroom. However, the teacher must take care to compare the student's performance with his scores on relevant abilities. A child may have a high intelligence test score and yet do very poorly in handwriting because he lacks hand-eye coordination. Or, a high school student who is average in quantitative reasoning capacity may earn high scores on ability tests that are biased in favor of verbal skills. It would be a mistake for the teacher to assume that this student should be accomplishing more in mathematics because of this verbal ability test score. In summary, if the teacher is to estimate the strength of a student's motivation to learn from the discrepancy between what he learns and what he is capable of learning, he must be certain that the measure of learning capability is adequate and relevant.

Another measure of the level of a student's motivation is based on changes in the quality of his performance, assuming that the requisite capacity remains about constant. To illustrate, suppose Mark has been performing in tenth-grade biology at a level which places him in the bottom third of the class during the first half of the school year. At Christmas his father gives him a microscope set and helps Mark become proficient in its use and the preparation of slides. The actual content of what he has learned as a result of this experience is not tested in the biology class, but an interest in biology has been aroused in Mark. During the second half of the year the teacher encourages Mark to show the class his slides and explain the technique used in making them. As a result of an increased interest in biology and the social rewards for his specific accomplishment, Mark spends much more time studying biology and is more attentive in the classroom. The change in his motivation results in his finishing the year as one of the top students in the biology class.

In this illustration, the teacher was able to detect a student's increased motivation by the change in his level of achievement relative to the lack of change in the level of achievement of the rest of the class. If the required work in the second half of the year had been easier than in the first half, the entire class might have seemed to have improved, but Mark's increased motivation could still be measured by comparing his improvement with that of the rest of the class. The quality of a student's performance sometimes will show a relative loss, instead of a gain, and thereby reveal to the teacher that some unfortunate set of circumstances has caused the pupil to be relatively less motivated than at an earlier time. Personal difficulties at home are one of many possible sources of a downward change in a student's eagerness to learn. Care must be taken to distinguish between *absolute* changes in motivation and *relative* changes. If the teacher uses a technique that increases the motivation of most of the students, the ones who are not changed in their *absolute* level of motivation will show a *relative* loss of motivation when compared to the others.

The teacher has many opportunities to form subjective impressions of a student's motivation to progress toward the goals that the teacher wishes him to obtain. When a student actively participates in class discussion, when he is eager to answer questions and to ask questions, the teacher can be reasonably confident that motivation is adequate and that there will be progress toward goals. Sometimes a student will spontaneously bring in materials related to class activities or will even ask how he may learn more about some topic. These positive reactions to the classroom experience give the teacher a clear picture of the student's motivation.

A student's failure to progress toward specific accomplishment may take two forms. When motivation is low, classroom symptoms include general apathy, looking out the window, daydreaming, and other states of inaction. The most striking element is not so much that the student is engaged in the wrong activities as it is that he seems inactive. At other times, students are motivated to engage in activities that conflict with classroom goals. Outside of school this may result in watching television and socializing with peers instead of doing homework. Within the classroom, motivation to win the approval of peers may produce behavior that disrupts the teaching-learning process. The unsatisfied social needs of a student may cause him to play the role of class clown, whisper, or even actively defy the teacher.

Although the distinction made here between the lack of motivation and competing motivation may be artificial, to the teacher there is a real, though subjective, difference. It is easy to ignore the apathetic student; as a result he often fails to receive attention while the unruly student tends to command first concern. With the apathetic student, the teacher's problem is to arouse motivation for movement toward classroom goals. With the obstreperous individual the problem is to rechannel their existing motivation; that is, the student with strong social needs must be given ways to satisfy these needs which are congruent with the goals of teaching. These new ways can be substituted for unacceptable forms of behavior directed at satisfying these same needs. Larry, who has a strong need for recognition and approval, has developed the trick of making funny noises in the back of the room. When the children laugh, he is reinforced for his efforts. It might be possible to give

Larry the social recognition he needs by giving him some leader-ship role in a discussion group or other activity. If he can receive the approval that he seeks in this way, he will gradually abandon his less legitimate tactics.

In using performance to form inferences about motivation, the teacher must remember that other factors besides low motiva-tion can interfere with performance. A student may be so eager to do well that his anxiety reduces his level of attainment. Or, especially in the early stages of learning, his motivation may be too high. As paradoxical as this may seem at first, it must be remem-bered that when students are beginning to learn, they will make more errors than they will later. If motivation is excessive, frustra-tion will result from the frequent unavoidable failures; anxiety will increase and further reduce the quality of performance. This problem is especially pronounced with young students.

Specific personality factors can also operate to give the errone-ous impression of low motivation. The individual may have the desire to reach some goal but be unable to initiate appropriate behavior for reasons other than lack of intellectual ability. Intro-version or shyness is a common problem in the classroom. Paul may have a strong desire to participate in some group activity—perhaps a discussion session—but be afraid that he will be ridi-culed or criticized for saying the wrong thing. The problem is not that he does not strongly desire to participate but that he has an equally strong or stronger motivation to avoid certain expected consequences of participation. The teacher should watch for indi-cations that conflicting motives exist and should not confuse conflicting motivation with lack of motivation. Symptoms of this type of conflicting motivation include anxiety, agitation, and behavior which alternates between approach of the desired goal and withdrawal from the situation. When there is high variability in a student's performance from day to day, it is likely that the problem is not simply lack of motivation, and the teacher should look for other causes.

CONFLICT IN THE CLASSROOM[1]

Conflict occurs when a person has more than one need and the satisfaction of one need requires that another be sacrificed. If one of the conflicting needs is much stronger, the conflict is quickly resolved in favor of satisfying the stronger need. But when the strength of conflicting needs are relatively comparable, problems arise. Some conflicts are caused by the existence of more than one attractive goal; others are the result of one goal possessing both positive and negative attributes.

FIGURE V.1. *Approach-Approach Conflict*

A conflict between two equally desirable goals is called an *approach-approach conflict*. In its simplest form, this is the easiest conflict to resolve. For instance, if a student must decide between two interesting books, he selects one or the other after only a moment's hesitation. The student receives immediate gratification and is assured that he will be able to have the other goal later (he can read the second book when he has finished the first). However, when the choice of one goal means giving up the other completely (as in the choosing of a career) and when the results of the choice are of long-range importance, the conflict becomes much more stressful. Two things must then occur in order for the conflict to be resolved; first, the individual must accept the fact—if it is indeed true—that he must choose one goal or the other and that it is not possible to obtain both. Second, the individual must decide which goal he really wants the most. This decision may involve teacher, parents, and counselors who can point out aspects of the situation which may not have occurred to the student. Sometimes students' conflicts are very quickly resolved when discussion reveals that they had misinformation or lacked knowledge of the consequences of one decision over another.

Other conflicts between desired goals are not so easily resolved. People often solve important conflicts on an irrational basis. For some reason they "feel" that one choice is superior. Later, they rationalize their decision by finding many reasons to justify their action. Since most conflicts have both conscious and unconscious components, what a person can verbalize may be misleading. The "real" source of a conflict can prove to be quite elusive and may only be revealed after many hours of intensive psychotherapy.

Here, however, we are primarily concerned with conflicts centering around the educational process. As was mentioned earlier, even when there is a positive attitude toward home study, it faces very strong competition. Few students can resist the temptation to be with their friends rather than put in extra time on their studies. This particular problem is resolved for many fortunate students by parents who are willing to help them make rules about when study will occur and its duration. Teen-agers and younger children are often saved a great deal of stress by the existence of rules set for them by adults. Many teen-age students are grateful for the rules set by teachers and parents, even though they express resentment at times. They are ambivalent about these rules, but they use them to resist peer-group pressures. When a student can tell his friends that he must leave because his parents expect him to be home at a certain time, he avoids the implication that he is leaving because he would rather study than be with them. The individual who is motivated both to maintain the approval of peers and to engage in activities that the peer group does not condone, feels a strong need for some sort of excuse that will let him do both.

APPROACH-AVOIDANCE CONFLICT

Often conflict arises because a goal has both positive and negative aspects. The individual is motivated to approach the goal, but at the same time he is motivated to avoid it. This form of conflict is termed an *approach-avoidance conflict*. The tendency to approach a goal is not the simple opposite of a tendency to avoid it. The strength of the tendency to approach a goal and the strength of the tendency to avoid it changes as a function of the distance from the goal. The tendency to approach can operate over very great distances. If you wanted to be with someone, the motivation to be with him could cause you to come great distances, perhaps from the other side of the world. But if you wanted to avoid, to be away from someone, you would feel no need to move to the other side of the world. The motivation to avoid does not move people over as great a distance as can the motivation to approach. This illustration uses *physical* distance, but distance from a goal may be *psychological* without any physical counterpart. A person's goal may be miles away, days away, or distant in that he has not yet brought himself to make certain decisions or take necessary actions to gain the goal. A person who wishes to be able to speak to large groups but is afraid to try is further from his goal, psychologically, than when he becomes willing to try to speak to small groups first, in order to build confidence. In this illustration, distance is not physical but rather "mental."

In an approach-avoidance conflict the individual first begins to approach the goal because approach tendencies operate over greater distance than do avoidance tendencies. As he approaches the goal, the tendency to avoid becomes stronger. If the individual

FIGURE V.2. *Approach-Avoidance Conflict*

FIGURE V.3. *Strength of Approach and Avoidance Tendencies as a Function of Distance from Goal*

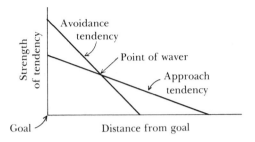

ceases to approach and wavers between approach and avoidance, he has reached a distance from the goal where the tendency to avoid has become stronger than the tendency to approach. The fact that wavering does occur, that people in conflict cease to approach a goal and show avoidance reactions, means that, by definition, avoidance has become stronger than approach. In order for avoidance to be stronger than approach near to the goal, the two tendencies must increase in strength at different rates. If the rate of change in strength of approach and avoidance were the same, the two tendencies would remain parallel; one or the other would be stronger at all distances from the goal, and the other tendency could never be stronger.

The behavior of both humans and animals fits the model of conflict illustrated in Figure V.3; that is, a model based on independent approach and avoidance motives that result in two tendencies differing in rate of change as a function of distance from the goal. A brief description of an animal experiment will illustrate that it is possible to show empirically that approach and avoidance differ in rate of change with distance from the goal. A hungry rat, with a harness attached to measure the strength with which he is moving, pulls harder when he is very near a food goal than when he is farther away. A frightened rat pulls harder to escape when he is near a source of pain than when he is farther away. The energy expended decreases faster with distance when avoiding than it increases with distance when approaching. A hungry rat that is punished and fed at the same location will approach until he reaches a point where his tendency to avoid pain becomes stronger than his tendency to reach food.

In the classroom, a child often finds himself in an analogous conflict. Perhaps the situation develops because an animal has been brought into the classroom as part of a nature lesson. All of the

FIGURE V.4. *If gradients of approach and avoidance were parallel, one would be stronger at all points.*

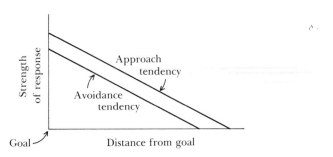

children are very excited, they crowd around the cage and are eager for a chance to touch the animal and participate in its care. At least, this is true of everyone except Linda. Several of the children notice that Linda is staying back some distance from the animal, and they encourage her to approach. The teacher may gently encourage her also, saying, "Linda. Would you like to come up closer so that you can see our new friend?" At first, no one realizes that Linda is terrified of the animal. Under mild encouragement, she moves slightly nearer the cage, but increasing fear soon stops her and she steps back again. This is a case of extreme approach-avoidance conflict. Linda wants to approach the animal the way the other children do, and she certainly wants to avoid having the others perceive her fear; but at the same time, her very real fear prevents her from reaching the goal. If the teacher is not perceptive, and if the children are allowed to tease Linda, the stress will increase. The problem may be understood in terms of increasing the tendency to approach without decreasing the tendency to

FIGURE V.5. *When the gradient of approach is raised, the intersection with the gradient of avoidance is at a higher level of avoidance.*

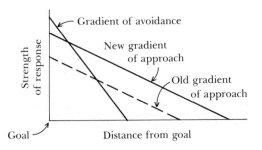

avoid. The tendency to avoid remains the same, but the increased approach gradient intersects the avoidance gradient at a point closer to the goal. Even though the individual has moved some toward the goal, he then enters on the avoidance gradient at a point where it is much stronger than before. The result is increased stress and heightened conflict.

Study of Figure V.6 suggests two ways in which an individual in an approach-avoidance conflict might eventually reach the goal. If the tendency to approach becomes stronger than the tendency to avoid at all distances, the individual would reach the goal but be under great stress because of the strong tendency to avoid. Or, if the tendency to avoid decreases until it is less than the tendency to approach at all points, the individual would be able to reach the goal.

The values of education do not make both solutions to approach-avoidance conflicts equally acceptable in the classroom. Students should not be subjected to excessive stress when an alternative exists. Extreme tension should be avoided not only because of humanitarian reasons but also because of the effect on attitude formation. If the classroom becomes associated with stress and unpleasant events, the child will strive to avoid school as much as possible. One way to resolve a conflict is to "leave the field," that is, to avoid the situation in which the conflict occurs. The young

FIGURE V.6. *There are two changes that can occur, either one of which will permit an individual to reach his goal in an approach-approach conflict.*

A. When the avoidance tendency becomes lower than the approach tendency at all points, the goal is reached with a minimum of anxiety.

B. When the approach tendency becomes higher than the avoidance tendency at all points, the goal is reached, but at the cost of great stress to the individual, because the tendency to avoid has not been reduced and it is greatest nearest to the goal.

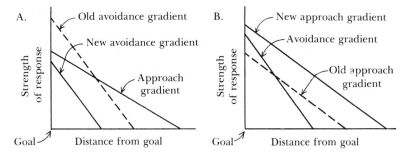

student cannot leave school, but he can have a high rate of absenteeism. He can learn to be "sick" in order to stay away. A suspiciously high rate of absenteeism should be noted by the teacher, and he should investigate the possibility that the missed days are a symptom of classroom difficulties.

When a student is in a strong approach-avoidance conflict, the teacher should not try to increase the tendency to approach the goal if it is at all possible to lower the tendency to avoid. The student is already under strong motivation to approach; if he were not, there would be no conflict. When the motivation for avoidance is reduced, the existing motivation to approach will take the student to the goal.

How can the teacher aid the student in the reduction of avoidance tendencies? Naturally, different situations will require custom-tailored treatment because of the circumstances, the personality of student and teacher, and the relative maturity of the student. However, it is possible to establish some general principles. When the conflict is caused by fear of a specific object—for example, the animal in our illustration—the fear can often be eliminated by allowing the student to become more familiar with the source of fear through indirect means. Linda could be given the opportunity to be the one who learns about the life habits of the animal and reports her findings to the class. Other possibilities might be to let her prepare its food or keep the weight records of its growth. Since it is the unknown aspects of a situation that are threatening, fear is often reduced by increased understanding. The process may be regarded as extinction of the fear response. The individual learns to deal with associated situations, finds them harmless, and his anxiety decreases. Once fear is reduced, the individual cautiously approaches the feared situation, nothing disastrous occurs, and his fear is still further reduced. In addition, there is the reward of successfully coping with a once dreaded conflict.

Another class of approach-avoidance conflicts is based on lack of confidence in the adequacy of one's performance. Whether it is speaking before the class, reading aloud, or volunteering for participation in an activity, some students will refrain because of a fear of failure and possible ridicule. Usually these students do want to participate and need opportunities to gain self-confidence. In order to prevent withdrawal, the student must know that the teacher will probably reward partial success.

Sometimes approach-avoidance conflicts arise because a student is asked to participate in an activity which is at variance with his self-concept. Boys will often rebel and resist taking on roles that they perceive as feminine or sissy. In some instances their objections are reasonable, while at other times they are not. Being in a play or acting out a part of a story is often avoided by boys who associate these activities with girls' games. Discussion of their television and movie heroes can often lead to the realization that these heroes are in fact men who have as their job the taking of parts and the playing of roles. As a result, the activity is perceived in a new way and becomes acceptable. The basic ingredient of this solution is to show the student that people he values endorse the activity.

DOUBLE APPROACH-AVOIDANCE CONFLICT

One of the most difficult and frequent conflicts in the classroom occurs when students feel a direct confrontation between the goals of the school and the values of their peer group. In high schools this may be seen in the strong fear of students that they may be considered "teacher's pet" by their fellows. This is an example of a *double* approach-avoidance conflict. There are two goals present—scholastic achievement and peer-group approval. Both goals possess both positive attributes and negative attributes. The negative attributes of each goal is the likelihood of losing the positive attribute of the other goal. (See Figure V.7.) There are several tactics often employed to avoid the stigma of peer-group disapproval. Sometimes students will intentionally make life difficult for the teacher through minor or even major acts of rebellion. Some bright students will make mistakes on purpose or give silly answers in class to win approval from their friends and demonstrate that they are not courting favor from the teacher. In some schools there is an unwritten taboo against "trying hard" to receive high grades. Often it is acceptable to do well in school as long as there is no evidence that energy is being expended for that purpose. The bright student can sometimes manage this subterfuge, but the average student is often hurt academically.

There is no easy answer to these problems. Resolution must involve a change in the student's perception of the school environment and the purposes of education. Research is needed to discover how to prevent the development of attitudes which lead students to perceive themselves as pitted in a struggle, with the teacher and the school against them. It is probably much more practical to prevent the development of these attitudes than to change them once they are formed. This is one reason why the early school years are so important.

There are certain policies the teacher can follow to minimize students' conflicts with their peer groups. The teacher should be alert to embarrassment resulting from excessive praise and other

FIGURE V.7. *Double Approach-Avoidance Conflict*

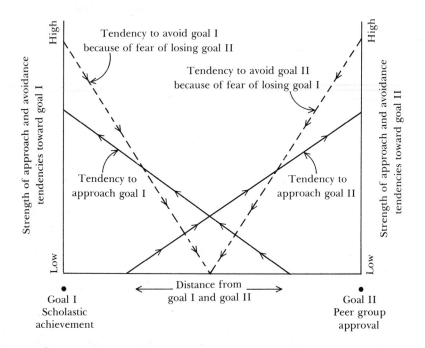

forms of singling out an individual with conspicuous attention. The adolescent's sensitivity presents difficulties easily overlooked by the teacher who is not empathic and perceptive. Without realizing what they are doing, adults are often as cruel to children as children are to each other. A little common sense can go a long way. There is no reason why the teacher should subject a boy to possible teasing by putting him in charge of watering the plants when the same job could be given to a girl. Conversely, moving chairs or leading in fire drills are acceptable to the young male student's concept of the masculine role.

Teachers sometimes unite the students in opposition by punishing the group for the transgressions of the individual. The practice is obviously unfair, and the students know it. General concepts of justice are learned very early, and fair play is a delicate issue with students.

Approach-avoidance conflicts may also arise over the making of career choices and graduation itself. Occasionally a student will be afraid of the consequences of graduation and will, without conscious intent, allow his work to slip in quality as though he actually wishes to fail. For some, the role of student is much more comfortable and secure than the unknown future that lies ahead. School counseling and guidance services should be enlisted when problems of this nature appear.

Another class of conflict—*avoidance-avoidance conflicts*—should be briefly noted. Sometimes an individual finds himself caught with two negative choices. The typical reaction is to leave the situation completely. When this is not possible there is acute stress. One example would be the student who does not want to study but at the same time does not want to fail. Another example would be the conflict of the child who is afraid to engage in some peer-group activity but also fears their ridicule.

Now that we have discussed the general concept of motivation we should consider specific aspects of this important factor in the classroom setting. One fundamental task of the teacher is to direct and maintain his students' attention to certain goals. Basically, the teacher has two assets in his attempt to increase the desire of the students to reach the goals valued by the school. He can provide the means for students to satisfy needs that already exist in ways that also satisfy the aims of the school. That is, the teacher can structure the path of learning in such a way that his students' existing needs are also gratified. In addition, the teacher can manipulate some variables in the school environment that bring about changes in the needs of the students.

Interests. If students are interested in what is occurring in the classroom, their attention will be directed toward the lesson rather than elsewhere. When a situation commands a person's attention, learning takes place. We often hear someone say, "Now pay attention to what I am saying." This plea is sometimes uttered by teachers who realize that they have not held the interest of the class and are trying to regain attention without having really earned it. When students are interested in a topic, they want to know more about the subject, and this intrinsic need can be satisfied only by learning.

People are interested in many different activities and subjects. Boys are interested in baseball, airplanes, and cars. Girls often show interest in adult female roles—mother, teacher, or nurse. Some interests are shared by many; others are more individual. One person may be interested in collecting and classifying sea shells, while someone else enjoys building scale-model ships. Whether interests are unique or shared by many, they function to direct the individual's activity and to maintain his attention.

The *existing interests* of the students can be valuable allies of the teacher. When an essay is written on "My Hobby" or "My Most Interesting Experience," there is going to be more individual involvement than when the teacher provides a specific topic. With younger learners, the opportunity to bring something that interests them to class and tell about it builds both self-confidence and expressive skills. "Show and Tell" is a common procedure in the early years of school, but in modified form the basic notion can be used with students of all ages. In high school, the specific interests of individuals can be topics for class presentations as well as essays. The imaginative teacher will find frequent opportunities to use the interests of the students as a medium for teaching material that would be somewhat dull otherwise. "If a rocket travels 18,000 miles per hour, how long will it take for it to go 100,000 miles?" The same problem, mathematically, would be far less interesting in another form. Specific interests also offer many possibilities for enrichment, including suggested additional reading and special projects.

The teacher quickly learns the group interests of students at the age level he is teaching. To the extent that the interests of boys and girls differ, both should be used in the classroom presentation. If the teacher is alert, he will detect new interests and ideas that have captured his students and incorporate these into his daily lesson plans. Because of the idiosyncratic nature of the relation between a given interest and course content, no rigid principle can, or should, be given. What can be said is that the teacher should seek ways to relate the interests of students to the material to be learned. If this is his intention, his natural ingenuity will supply him with the method in any given situation.

In the teaching of reading, it is very important to use material that is interesting and exciting. Many bright learners rebel against the triteness of the stories they read and will even complain, "People don't really talk that way!" If a story is worth while, the students will want to read it in order to know the outcome. When students who are learning to read seem uninterested in knowing a story's conclusion, the choice of reading selections should be re-examined.

Students of all ages are interested in adult roles and value the opportunity to make decisions that they associate with having full status in our society. History becomes much more interesting when a student must decide what he would have done if he had been the general or president faced with a particular problem. The opportunity to assume roles, including the role of teacher, involves students in a way that can never be accomplished when they are forced to assume a passive part in the teaching-learning process. When students are interested in an activity or a topic, the activity or topic is, by definition, meaningful to them.

Thus far, we have discussed the use of existing interests in the teaching-learning process. It is also possible to create new interests as a result of classroom experiences which will then motivate students as much as previously existing interests. The specific interests of one student will often capture the imagination of others if he is given an opportunity to share his ideas. The teacher of an elementary school class will find that setting up an aquarium of frogs in various stages of metamorphosis will arouse strong interest. The children will want to know many things, and the teacher will be able to tie in topics of growth and development, practice in observation, and comparative studies. Some students will already know a fair amount about frogs and will be very eager to share their knowledge. Field trips to farms, factories, or courts also create interests that will maintain involvement in many diverse classroom activities.

Interests can be aroused by concepts as well as by concrete objects. An idea suggested by the teacher can result in enthusiastic involvement. When children try to name "things that are round" or "things made of metal," they become very interested in the concept of sets and the opportunity for creativity of thought. In high school, laboratory demonstrations in physics and chemistry can arouse interests, especially when the phenomenon has relevance for everyday life. Inertia illustrated by the problem of the racing driver when he must corner his car is more meaningful to most boys than more abstract or artificial examples. Since there is a degree of freedom when choosing illustrations of a concept, the teacher should consider the attention-arousing potential of possible alternatives. When preparing lesson plans, he can add marginal notes that will provide him with selected examples rather than depend completely on spontaneous intuition in the classroom.

There is an intimate relation between interests and curiosity. When students become curious about a phenomenon in science or the outcome of some problem in current events, their interest is maintained and their behavior will be directed toward satisfying their curiosity. There is much yet to be learned about the nature of curiosity, but in some ways it seems to be an innate rather than a learned predisposition. It is important that the curiosity of students be satisfied and rewarded or the tendency to inquire will be diminished. When children come from homes where questions were not answered or were considered to be a nuisance, the teacher must patiently restore the natural predisposition to be curious and develop the attitude that inquiry will be rewarded. Students should be praised for a "good question" as much as for a right answer. Positive reinforcement of thoughtful inquiry can produce a classroom atmosphere that is far more interesting than one where passive response is the rule.

Manipulation. Akin to curiosity is the desire of people to manipulate, to operate upon, the environment around them. Students are interested in handling objects, performing experiments, and controlling the outcome of a situation. In art class, the desire to knead the clay oneself is not too different from the desire in chemistry class to perform an experiment without direct assistance. Educators could profit from observing teen-age boys playing a pinball machine; interest, rapt attention, and the joy of manipulation come together to produce behavior bordering on obsessive-compulsive involvement. Whenever possible, students should be allowed to engage in experiments, build models related to the lesson theme, and experience things directly as well as in abstract discussion. For a child in the inner city who has never seen a frog, a picture is a sorry substitute for the sensation of holding the living creature.

The teacher should be constantly alert for the opportunity to provide direct sensory experiences for his students. This is possible even in the most abstract of the disciplines—mathematics. When students can handle geometric solids or manipulate counters, their motivation to have further related experiences is increased. In the selection of visual and tactual aids to education, the teacher would do well to consider the possibilities of each device in terms of direct physical use by students. A teaching device that is manipulated by students commonly produces far more motivation than purely visual displays.

Novelty and Motivation. People are motivated to participate in new activities that are different from their previous experiences. Without doubt, curiosity is a basic component of the reaction to novelty. Even though the material is novel, students sometimes become bored because the method of instruction is not. A new teaching method may appear to be intrinsically better than an older method because it produces better results, but the real advantage may simply be that it is new. When the novelty effect has worn off, the new method may prove to be less worthy than the traditional way. This effect presents a difficult problem for educational research when a new technique is compared with one to which the students are already accustomed. Only after the new technique has been in use for a prolonged time is it possible to render an accurate evaluation.

There is nothing wrong with capitalizing on the novelty effect in order to motivate students. Variety in demonstrations, audio-visual materials, and classroom activities maintain student interest and reduce the likelihood of boredom from constant repetition. Also, it is very important for students to develop the attitude that the classroom is a place where exciting and interesting events take place. This does not mean that the teacher must produce an array of original activities for every lesson, but rather that novelty should be introduced when possible and allowed to serve as one of the many forms of reinforcement for being in the school environment. The teacher can always ask himself two questions: "Is there some new way in which I can present this material in order to make it more meaningful and more interesting? What activities, demonstrations, movies, etc., would enrich the classroom presentation and direct attention to the important elements?" The teacher should also remember that once he discovers ways to arouse interest and enthusiasm in his class, he will be able to use these ideas again the following year, since they will be new and fascinating to a different class.

THE NEED TO ACHIEVE

The need to achieve seems to vary from one individual to the next. The need to achieve may be regarded as a personality trait that is manifested in a desire to be successful or to win in any activity undertaken. The specific activity is not too critical; the individual with a strong need to achieve strives for success whether he is in a race, playing chess, studying for a test, or pursuing a career. For him, an activity is an opportunity for achievement rather than something of intrinsic worth. Failure in any endeavor is far more distressing to the achiever than it is for the individual who receives some intrinsic rewards for participation. A high level of aspiration is typical of people with strong achievement needs. They set high goals for themselves and strive hard to realize these goals.

Studies indicate that early parental pressure for independence and accomplishment is a prime factor in developing a need to achieve. Parents of an only child expect and encourage him to attain certain levels of maturity and acquire skills earlier than do other parents, and they constantly reward achievement with praise and affection, and press for still further progress. This treatment produces a strong need for achievement in the child which can become a permanent part of his personality. The tendency for parents to press for early achievement varies with the education, religion, and socioeconomic level of the parents.

David McClelland, who has studied human motivation extensively, has shown that the need to achieve even enters the individual's fantasy life and can be measured there.[2] In the Thematic Apperception Test a person is shown a number of pictures and is asked to make up a story based on each one. Clinical psychologists use this test to measure people's needs and problems by the way in which they project them into the stories they tell. Individuals with a strong need to achieve produce stories in which achievement is a dominant theme. For example, one picture shows a boy with a violin resting on a table in front of him. Most people tell a story having to do with the boy's dislike of violin lessons and how he would rather be outside playing baseball. A person with high achievement needs, however, may make up a story in which the boy is dreaming about becoming a great violinist and then go on to describe how the boy studies constantly for many years, overcoming all obstacles, and finally achieves his goal. Research has shown that those individuals who emphasize achievement in their fantasy do, in fact, achieve more than others and strive to accomplish tasks that others tend to abandon when success is not immediate. Of course, some individuals achieve only in their fantasies and accomplish nothing in the real world. Even in their fantasies, these people tend to emphasize "magical" devices rather than effort. They dream of "suddenly" acquiring skills and status, while the true achiever is more likely to imagine the rewards he will someday gain as a result of his endeavor.

The need to achieve is an important determinant of performance in school and in later life. Some students, and even whole classes of students, have such a need to achieve that the teacher does not have to be concerned about producing motivation. Everyone has seen the child who literally vibrates with eagerness to answer every question, participates in all activities, and even welcomes the homework assignment as another opportunity to achieve. When teaching these very highly motivated students, the teacher should not overlook certain problems. For instance, the need to achieve unfortunately often outstrips the capacity to achieve. This simple imbalance accounts for a large proportion of human frustration and discontent. Whether a person's need for achievement is high or low, he should be encouraged to strive for goals which are reasonable, that is, obtainable for him given his ability. Even the highly motivated child will attempt projects beyond his ability if the teacher does not adroitly intervene and guide him into a wiser form of endeavor. Another problem is that the achievement-driven student tends to become involved in so many activities that the quality of all the activities is sacrificed. If the teacher is alert to these pitfalls, he can give the student appropriate guidance.

In general, competition is a pervasive and valued part of our society. It is felt that competition, in the form of free enterprise, leads to the highest individual rewards and the most acceptable plan for improving the condition of everyone's way of life. A store succeeds because it sells a better product or sells at a lower price, and men succeed when they perform better than others who are in the same profession. Competition extends beyond both school and occupation and becomes a fundamental component of many aspirations. Keeping up with or, better yet, exceeding the Joneses is a driving force for many people. It becomes important to have a larger house, a newer car, and brighter children who do better in school.

Some argue that competition is fundamental and point to natural selection and the survival value of aggressiveness and willingness to compete. Others point out cultures where there seems to be little or no competition between individuals. The people of the Samoan Islands, for example, strive for communal goals rather than for individual aggrandizement. However, the existence of non-competitive cultures and individuals proves little, because learned inhibition of natural competitive behavior could cause the lack of competition.

Competing with Others in the Classroom. The important question at the moment has to do with the way competition functions in the classroom. Students compete for the attention and approval of the teacher, but the major issue which has concerned education is competition between students for grades, gold stars, and other symbols of achievement, such as being placed on the honor roll. The problem must be approached in the context of the value systems which exist in our schools and our society.

Some argue that since a person in our culture must function in a competitive environment, it would be unwise and misleading to shelter students from competition while in school. The argument leads to the proposition that if the child does not learn to compete with others in school, he will be helpless when he leaves school and enters the "real world." Upon closer analysis, this justification of competition in the classroom proves to be inadequate. Children of all ages have enough opportunity to compete with their peers and their siblings outside of the classroom. Most games are competitive, both the formal games purchased for children and the games they devise themselves. All forms of competition are presented to the child in the television programs he watches and in the stories he reads or has read to him. There may be some merit to competition in the classroom under certain conditions, but it cannot be justified on the basis that the child must learn it there or suffer later.

There are several serious consequences of encouraging competition in order to motivate performance that the teacher must avoid. Competition tends to produce high rates of performance at the expense of the quality of the production. Students easily confuse quantity with quality. It is important for the teacher to consistently reward quality in order to help the students learn the distinction. Excessive competition is bad for the young child who has not learned to handle it and who may quickly become frustrated. He may develop undesirable attitudes or resort to cheating in order to do better than others when legitimate strategies are not available.

Many of these complications arise because competition usually helps those who are already the better performers. Competition also has little to offer when the prize is not worth the effort or the activity is repugnant; for example, boys will not compete for a prize in an activity they view as feminine.

Competition between teams can be used to advantage in some situations since no one stands alone as a loser. The teams should be arbitrary and should be changed each time to prevent emphasis on being the member of a particular team. For example, girls against boys in a spelling game should be avoided. Instead, a red team and blue team could be formed by random assignment. The successful involvement of competition motives in the classroom requires the use of strategies which do not limit the number of winners and which are intrinsically interesting so that competition does not dominate the activity.

Competing Against Past Performance. A very useful motive is the desire to improve relative to one's own past performance. Obvious examples include the golfer or bowler who remembers his best game and constantly tries to better his score. This is not the same as competition against others, which requires group interaction with winners and losers, or at least relative losers. A person competing against his own past performance has a reasonable expectation of success since he need only do a little better than the best he already knows he is capable of doing. The teacher can promote this motive by rewarding students for improvement. Even though the absolute level of his performance is not high, the student should receive praise and approval for the fact that his performance represents an improvement over his past level of attainment. The teacher should not give the impression that the absolute level is good if in fact it is not. The approval should be explicitly attached to the improvement. For the insecure student, improvement is perceived as a much more attainable goal than some absolute level of achievement that seems remote. If samples of a student's work are retained, he may be shown his improvement, which is more impressive to him than simply being told that he is doing better. Since all students can improve, there need be no losers in this form of competition. The basic attitude that additional effort will produce improved results is an essential ingredient of success both in school and later in the pursuit of a career. The simple conviction that one can do better by trying can result in improvement in academic attainment as well as in motor skills such as typing, dancing, and athletics.

THE NEED TO CONFORM TO GROUP STANDARDS

An individual in our society is rewarded for thinking and behaving in the same manner as his associates. It is very important to students that they not be different from their peers in behavior, in clothing, or in many other ways. They feel secure in their group identification and are threatened by any possibility of alienation. Conformity has, unfortunately, taken on some negative connotations. When a person is described as a "conformist," an image is aroused which includes rigidity, conventionality, and lack of imagination. Actually it is possible and desirable for an individual to conform in some ways but not in others. A man can obey the law, conform to social mores, and still be a creative scientist whose work is completely original. Similarly, it is not inconsistent for the teacher to press for conformity to some standards and encourage originality and independence at other times. In this way students learn to discriminate situations where creative originality is valued.

Conformity drives facilitate the teaching-learning process when individual students are motivated to participate in classroom activities because their fellow students are participating. A child who would be difficult to motivate in isolation will often perform because of group influence. Many teachers notice that when students are working on individual tasks at their desks, there is a positive effect from the fact that their peers are similarly occupied. Students working in isolation are not as productive. Another form of social support for activity occurs when one student works at the chalkboard while others work at their desks. The fact that one of their peers is conspicuously working away at some problem maintains the other students' efforts. In fact, the student working in sight of the class at the front of the room functions as a "pacesetter." If he is industrious, there is a contagious effect upon the rest of the pupils.

As was noted earlier, conformity needs can operate in opposition to the teaching-learning process when the social code of the students conflicts with the requirements of the classroom. This problem is rare in the earliest years of school but can be a definite problem in junior high and high school. Often the problem is one of misunderstanding due to inadequate communication between teacher and students. If the teacher perceives group opposition to any of his policies or the requirements of the school, he should try to determine the exact nature of the conflict. As often as not, some resolution can be found that both preserves the values of the school and permits the students to feel that they are being treated fairly.

THE NEED TO BE EGO-INVOLVED

When a person invests self, *ego,* in a situation, he is very highly motivated to work for a satisfactory conclusion or result. Where there is strong identification with an activity, failure will be taken as personal failure. Sporting events often produce extreme ego-involvement; it is difficult to be a "good loser" when one's self-concept is threatened.

High school and college students often regard their intelligence as a very important asset. For this reason failure in intellectual activities can be most threatening. Sometimes students will intentionally not try to perform at their highest level. This strategy provides a rationalization for failure. If a student tries to do well in school, he is often left with no excuse for poor grades other than personal inadequacy, which is defeating to his ego.

Although the teacher wants his students to take pride in their work, he should also help them avoid excessive involvement, especially with younger students who have not yet learned to view the world in proper perspective. There is a subtle difference between saying "You did not do well" and "This paper could be improved considerably." The information given the student is the same, but the latter statement criticizes the performance rather than the individual. When a task or project is worthy of heavy personal involvement, the teacher should encourage students' investment and at the same time provide for success. Some teachers make the mistake of trying to get students to take a personal stake in everything they do, even when the probability of success is low.

THE NEED FOR SELF-ACTUALIZATION OR REALIZATION

Students are highly motivated to achieve goals that are consistent with their self-concept. Self-actualization[3] is used here to denote a special determinant of ego-involvement where the individual is motivated to make his image of what he might accomplish come true. A boy will practice catching a baseball for hours. He is motivated by the desire to acquire a skill that he believes he is capable of acquiring. If he did not believe he could reach that goal, he would not be motivated to practice.

The role of self-confidence in this aspect of motivation is obvious. If a person does not believe he is capable of improving his academic performance, he will not try. When the teacher can show his students that certain goals are within their reach, they can accept the goals and are motivated to achieve them in order to actualize their new self-concept.

CLASSROOM VARIABLES THAT AFFECT MOTIVATION

GRADES AND MOTIVATION

Under certain circumstances students are motivated to perform classroom activities and to study at home in order to receive high grades, gold stars, or other symbolic rewards. Grades possess some of the attributes of good motivational devices, but at the same time they present some serious problems. It is true that grades do set a goal for the student (a characteristic of most adequate techniques for producing motivation) but, unfortunately, the goal is often remote and also tends to be extrinsic to the values of education.

A grade that comes at the end of a term or other long span of time does not serve as useful feedback for the monitoring of ongoing performance. Grades also tend to be nonspecific; that is, the grade conveys the general information that performance was excellent, adequate, or poor but does not indicate exactly what was wrong or what was well done. Does a low grade in history represent failure to learn certain facts, failure to organize the facts, or lack of imagination in perceiving interrelations? If grades are to be useful they must be frequent, and they must be accompanied by clear explanations of their meaning. Frequent grades are not too important for the college student because he knows whether or not he is mastering the material to be learned, but elementary and high school students have had less experience in self-appraisal and need more feedback.

Grades can motivate students to further effort by providing an objective knowledge of results. Too often, however, grades become a source of competition in the classroom, and they take on special meaning extrinsic to the task of learning. Cheating on tests is a clear indication that the grade is what is valued, not the acquisition of knowledge or skills. Instead of motivating the student, grades sometimes have a demoralizing effect. For example, when the teacher grades on the "curve," automatically giving low grades to the students with the lowest level of performance regardless of their absolute attainment or performance, students who consistently receive low marks may come to believe that they are incapable of doing anything better.

Parents are often at fault in making their children grade-conscious. However, it is hard to blame them alone when grades are so highly valued by colleges when choosing between applicants. The schools, parents, and colleges must find a way to place the emphasis on grades *qua* grades in a more reasonable perspective. One solution might be to search for a feasible way to base college admission on standardized achievement and aptitude tests to a greater extent than is now practiced. The reason colleges concern themselves with a student's high school grades is that these are the best single predictor of grades in college. High school performance can reflect an adequate combination of ability and motivation to succeed academically, while most college entrance exams do not reflect the student's capacity for sustained academic effort. In other words, performance is the best predictor of performance. The development of really adequate measures of ability, achievement, and motivation could serve to reduce the strength of the grade fetish.

Another shortcoming of grades is that they are quite susceptible to what is called the *halo effect*. Students who are quiet and well behaved tend to receive higher grades than those who are more obstreperous. Although teachers do not consciously bias the grades they give, they are influenced by factors unrelated to what should be judged. Another example of the halo effect would be a student's being given a low grade on a history essay because of poor handwriting while a student who typed his paper receives a higher grade even though the knowledge of history revealed by the essays is identical.

TESTS AND MOTIVATION

Tests and examinations not only provide an indirect measure of learning, but they also set up conditions which will produce learning because students are motivated to study when they know a test is imminent. Unfortunately, people tend to procrastinate, and the days before an exam are often filled with feverish preparation that should have been spread over a greater span of time. "Surprise" tests seem to have little merit in the production of study motivation, since it is easy for students to convince themselves that "Surely there will not be a test tomorrow because. . . ." The optimum frequency of tests for purposes of motivation varies with the maturity of students. In high school, tests about every two weeks appear optimal, while with younger or slower students more frequent testing seems desirable. The teacher should consider the possible implication of the form and emphasis of a test. When students take a test, they learn what the teacher considers to be important, and they orient their future preparation accordingly. If a given test is biased in its emphasis, the students may then concentrate on learning material in the direction of this bias. In high schools and colleges, the author has observed one very effective technique for increasing the likelihood that students will concentrate on the important facets of a subject. This technique consists of giving the students twelve essay questions a reasonable amount of time before the test. They are told that three of the questions will constitute the test. The students know what to study, and the teacher knows that in preparing each question the students will learn important material in addition to the items which appear on the test itself. This technique may be used with modifications for examinations other than the essay variety.

SOURCES OF REDUCED MOTIVATION

We should not leave the discussion of motivation without touching upon some specific causes of reduced effort. Many of these are obvious. Boredom, frustration, and fatigue will naturally prevent a student from achieving at his optimum level. The factors that can produce these forms of interference have been considered in different contexts throughout this book. Also, there should be no need to elaborate the fact that if the room is uncomfortably warm, if the students are hungry, or if it is the day before vacation, the students will direct less attention toward classroom activities.

Sometimes the motivation of students is reduced because they are dissatisfied with their progress. When effort does not result in improvement, students, especially younger ones, will quickly accept defeat and not expend further effort. One cause of the feeling of "no progress" is the fact that performance during learning does not improve at a steady rate. Plateaus are common in learning a skill. One explanation is that an integration process is active during this time and lower order skills are being organized into higher order skills. After a person learning to type masters the location of the letters, he may experience no improvement for a while and then begin to type at higher level because he is thinking in terms of words rather than individual letters. The same phenomenon is often seen in the learning of reading or the development of motor

FIGURE V.8. *The course of learning often includes "plateaus" or periods of little improvement.*

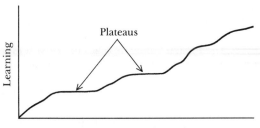

skills, e.g., swimming or tennis. The teacher should be aware that this is a natural aspect of learning and encourage the student who has reached a plateau to continue his efforts.

One of the most important factors, if not *the* most important factor, in reduced motivation is the distance between the individual and his goal. The problem is not unique to any age, nor is it confined to the classroom. Simply stated, goals are often psychologically too distant to sustain effort at the present. Many college freshmen complain that they are not motivated to study and that their grades are suffering as a result. After intensive academic effort in high school to gain entrance into college, their next major goal seems to be four years away. It is essential that they learn to accept and work for closer goals—the next test or, better yet, the mastery of a certain body of material.

For the young learner, the problem is similar but different in some important aspects. Because he has learned to mediate between the present and the future, the experienced individual can accept more distant goals than can the young child. An adult can think about distant goals and tell himself that his present effort is worth the eventual reward. The child has not yet acquired this point of view and as a result requires more immediate goals. He also needs a high degree of confidence that he has the capacity to be successful. The teacher must provide incentives that possess both of these qualities. A central difficulty is that the real reasons we want a child to acquire certain skills are not adequate reasons to him. Our values are related to needs and accomplishments that are far removed in time from the experiences of the early grades.

A child will not learn to read because he *must* in order to learn the content of the various disciplines, to gain entrance into college, or to be able to compete in a literate society. His is largely the world of the present, or, at most, the very near future. A child will learn to read, or for that matter learn anything else, only when the goals are very close to him in time. Often the teacher of reading depends upon developing interest in the outcome of a particular story to motivate the children to continue reading. The illustrations in the reader are used in a similar manner. "Look! Tom's ball has rolled into the river. Let us read the rest of the story and find out if he is able to get it back." If the children are curious, they will attempt to read the story. However, if they find the plot uninteresting, their motivation may be quite low. Many children have come to dislike reading because of the banal material offered to them. When this happens, the teacher obviously should substitute selections.

In our discussion of motivation, we have considered many factors that can cause the learner's attention to be directed toward goals valued by the school. The entire question is, in essence, "How can the attention of the learner be directed to the right goals and how can this attention, once earned, be maintained?" It is to be hoped that a great deal more research and speculation will be directed toward the phenomenon of attention. What we already know about this variable is very useful in the classroom; what we must yet discover is considerable and very important to the discipline of education.

•

CHAPTER SIX

Methods

of

Teaching

•

It is not enough for a teacher to want his students to learn the fundamental concepts of physics, biology, history, or any other discipline. He must also have the capacity and ability to achieve his goal. The noblest of goals will not produce results unless there is some method or process that will enable the learners to move toward that goal. For the purposes of the present discussion, we can define a teaching method as a repeatable way of teaching, repeatable not only in the sense that one teacher can use the same way of teaching on different occasions but also in the sense that other teachers can learn to employ the technique. Some methods of teaching may be used in many different disciplines. The lecture method, for example, is used to teach chemistry, biology, history, and a great array of other subjects. Other methods may be specific to the subject content—for instance, a method of teaching reading or of teaching arithmetic.

A successful teaching method must include more than a simple presentation of the material to be learned. To be successful, a method must produce the learning sought by the teacher. But this alone is not enough; as we have seen earlier, there are several other essential considerations. What is learned must be learned in a form that can be transferred outside the classroom or to the learning of other material.

A teaching method may appear to be successful by most measures, but still produce undesirable and harmful side effects. We have discussed the ways in which forms of learning that are not part of the explicit goals of learning can occur. There is incidental learning of attitudes toward the subject matter, the teacher, and the education process itself. A method of teaching history may produce the learning intended by the teacher, but it may, in addition, generate negative attitudes toward future study. For instance, students often express very strong feelings against particular subjects even though there was sufficient extrinsic motivation, e.g., grades, to cause them to learn the material.

The teaching methods employed by educators determine part of the environment of the school. Students adjust to this environment with varying degrees of success depending, in part, on the nature of the environment. Successful teaching methods produce an environment in which both the goals and values of education are preserved. At the same time, that environment must be one in which the students can be motivated to engage and feel that they have reasonable assurance of success.

Earlier we defined teaching as causing to learn. This broad approach permitted consideration of aspects of the influence of one individual upon another which are both intentional and unintentional—intentional, as when a teacher consciously tries to impart a principle of physics to his students, and unintentional, as with much of attitude transmission.

Historically, there has always been the form of teaching represented by the influence of parents upon the behavior of their children. We can only speculate about the origins of the *intent* to teach. Perhaps it began when fathers first took pride in their sons and endeavored to impart to them those skills that would earn credit for the fathers in the clan or tribe. The first approximation to formal group instruction may have been puberty initiations and the introduction of the young into adult society. At any rate, formal teaching, including *classes*, began long before there were written records to document its development.

TRADITIONAL TEACHING METHODS

One source of teaching methods employed by teachers today is the reservoir of techniques that have been in use for many years. The traditional methods were not deliberately developed to cope with a particular aspect of the psychology of learning; instead they were developed through the long history of teacher-student relations. However, the basic psychological factors in the teaching-learning process have always existed and still remain. The traditional methods have had to provide the prerequisites for human learning in order to be successful; and they have been relatively successful. They have not only provided an adequate education for masses of people in the past but endure today as the basic techniques of formal education. It is important to examine both their origin and the manner in which they deal with the diverse problems of human learning that receive unequal emphasis when highly specialized techniques are used.

Most teaching-learning relationships involve more than one teaching method. However, if we examine a small segment of the total process, we often find that the activities at that moment can be defined. Since all of the possible modifications make it difficult to label exactly the point at which one method becomes transformed into another, it should be remembered that most of the classifications are arbitrary and made for purposes of discussion.

LECTURE METHOD

A lecture is a formal discourse intended for instruction. The original meaning of the term was "to read,"[1] but today the usage is more general and refers to a verbal presentation by the teacher of the material to be learned. By using the lecture method, the teacher is able to present exactly the material he chooses in the way he prefers. The lecture in pure form is marked by a lack of discussion or interaction between teacher and students, although sometimes the lecture is followed by a discussion session in which the students question the teacher. In college, a professor will sometimes give formal lectures to quite large classes without discussion, but even then, the students often meet later in small groups with instructors who answer questions about the professor's presentation.

In elementary school and high school, teachers lecture for shorter periods of time than in college. They describe a chemical process, a physics phenomenon, or an historical episode. The brief lecture is then followed by a thorough discussion. The lecture technique should be used in very brief sessions with younger learners—a few minutes at a time—because they are easily bored and distracted if not given opportunities for active participation. The danger of losing the attention of students is reduced when a lecture is accompanied by demonstrations or other interesting supplements.

There are several ingredients in a successful lecture technique. An adequate speaking voice is, of course, essential, but the teacher must also say something interesting and meaningful. In addition, he must use a comprehensible vocabulary, and his presentation must possess logical continuity. Fortunately, frowns and questions usually provide feedback to the teacher when his lecture is not clear.

When used in longer sessions with older students, the lecture often reveals how the teacher thinks about a problem. He can show which facts and theories he believes to be relevant, and the students can witness the intellectual development of a concept. Instead of giving a formal lecture with no interruptions, the teacher may allow the students to raise their hands to indicate that they do not understand or to make individual contributions. For example, a tenth-grade biology teacher may be giving a brief description of the distinction between miosis and mitosis. After this "lecture" has continued for several minutes, one student asks a question. The answer to the question leads to further questions, and discussion spontaneously replaces lecture as the central method of instruction. Flexibility of teaching method is important; skillful teaching occurs when one approach, or one method, is abandoned at the most propitious moment for the introduction of a different teaching technique.

To be successful, all teaching methods must direct the attention of students toward the important elements and the critical relationships to be learned. This task is more difficult with the lecture method because of the reduced interaction between teacher and students. The teacher cannot be positive that the students are concentrating on the important points or, for that matter, concentrating at all. If the lecture builds toward the central points without digression, the attention of students will be properly directed. This is not difficult when the topic has intrinsic interest; in other situations, the topic must be made interesting through the way in which it is presented.

Consider two different presentations of the same material to a biology class: In one class the teacher begins, "In plants there is a variety of mechanisms that permit the maintenance of life systems. Some plants are parasitic, while others trap live organic forms. Most plants, of course, depend upon water soluble foods that can be obtained through their root systems." In another classroom, the teacher starts with a rhetorical question, "Are there any man-eating plants? No, there are not, but there are plants that capture small insects, just as a spider does with his web." After describing how these plants trap insects, the teacher develops the concept that plants have life requirements just as animals do. The same information will be offered in both presentations; but the latter approach will hold the attention of the students, while the pedantry of the first approach will produce boredom and frustration. The teacher must orient his presentation in a way that is compatible with the interests and ability of the students.

Since many teachers allow discussion during a lecture, there is no real point at which a clear distinction can be drawn. As used here, discussion is characterized by two-way verbal interaction between teacher and students or between students. The research evidence does not indicate large differences in content learning between lecture and discussion methods when students are tested shortly after the lecture or discussion. Research on long-term retention and other parameters of learning also gives meager support to the superiority of either method. However, the effectiveness of discussion has been revealed by practical experience in the classroom. For example, discussion possesses elements known to be important in motivation and the maintenance of interest. Perhaps the most important aspect of group discussion as a teaching method is that it involves the active participation of the students in the teaching-learning process. Students enjoy an opportunity to express their opinions, and when they know that they can contribute, they direct their attention toward the classroom activity more than when learning is a passive experience. With only passive participation, the students' attention can easily drift away from the learning situation.

Discussion can follow, or be integrated with, a wide range of activities. A field trip, a film, an experiment, or a demonstration are a few of the learning experiences that can lead to open discussion. At other times, discussion occurs spontaneously as the result of someone's contribution to the group or of a problem that arises. Occasionally, the class will become interested in some topic that is not directly related to the material which the teacher has planned to use. Under these circumstances, the teacher has to decide whether or not the class interest can be related to the planned material. If it can, the teacher should make use of the motivation that exists because of the students' interest. If the topic of class interest is quite remote, the teacher must decide whether to pursue the topic or, instead, guide the discussion back to the original subject. With a highly involved group that constantly introduces tangential topics, the teacher may decide that the particular idea introduced should not be followed at the present time. But if the class is one that tends to be low in motivation, it may be worth while to pursue a line of discussion that captures the students' imagination, even though it is a departure from the intended lesson. It is quite rewarding for students to discuss a subject that they initiate. Among other things, it increases their tendency to perceive the school as a source of satisfaction for their curiosity.

One difficulty with discussion as a teaching method—which is shared by most other methods—is the student who does not participate. The teacher soon finds that some students are always ready to join into a discussion, whereas others seldom, if ever, take part. Pressing the reluctant student rarely solves the problem. Often the withdrawn student is afraid he will say something wrong, and he does not want to run the risk of possible ridicule. One approach to the situation is to divide the class into several small discussion groups. After each group has prepared a presentation of the topic, one spokesman from each group then shares the conclusion of his group with the rest of the class. By exercising some care in the composition of the groups, the teacher can increase the probability that all students will have an opportunity to contribute. For example, the most hesitant student should not be placed in a group with a very extroverted individual who would overwhelm him. After a student develops confidence in small-group interaction, he can then begin to participate in activities that involve the entire class.

One of the most effective techniques for promoting group discussion is some form of the Socratic method of questioning. The teacher can say, "I wonder why tires are made from rubber instead of something else?" Such a question will usually arouse the interest of many students and cause them to offer their opinions. Once the first students reply, a sort of social facilitation occurs, and others are motivated to contribute to the group. In effect, they want to be part of the group, and they perceive that it is necessary to enter the discussion in order to be included.

One advantage of group discussion is the possibility of constant feedback between teacher and students. When a response is erroneous or inappropriate, immediate modification can be introduced and justified, whereas with most other methods the feedback is delayed and the learner is allowed to believe that his performance is adequate until some time later. Another advantage of discussion is that it is very flexible. If some tangent arouses interest, it can be pursued; or, if certain points prove to be confusing, discussion can resolve the difficulty. To be successful, however, discussion does require a skillful teacher as well as preparation on the part of the students.

Group discussion can be very important in the area of attitude development and modification. The social context is the source of this strength. When one sees how one's peers feel about an issue and listens to their arguments, the desire to identify with the group leads to a desire to understand its position on an issue. The teacher is often perceived as a source of authority too similar to that of the parent, and some degree of resistance to his position is aroused. But when new ideas and sentiments come from the peer group, a student is less defensive and more inclined toward favorable response, although some students conform to the norms of their group more than others.

The project method is not really a specific method. Rather, it is a general name for the form of the teaching-learning process that consists of students' working on some task with relatively little direct interaction with the teacher. The specific project may be assigned by the teacher or may result from student initiative. With younger students, it is better to provide highly structured tasks, such as directing them to color in a map to show the principal industries of different states or the various countries. Naturally, less mature students require more guidance from the teacher. Older students should be encouraged to plan and develop projects on their own which are related to the current theme of the classroom. For some students, guidance can be minimal and often will consist only of encouraging reasonable projects; that is, the teacher can help students to select projects that they can realistically expect to bring to a satisfactory conclusion. Only experience with the particular students to be taught can provide an answer to the question of how much guidance is appropriate.

Projects are also valuable in that they promote the development of the capacity for self-reinforcement, which is so important in later life. The individual takes pride in the fact that the project is *his*, and he is additionally motivated by the realization that the teacher expects him to do a good job and has expressed confidence in his capacity to handle the task on his own. Additional reinforcement results when the final product of a project is displayed in some manner or presented to the class.

A project need not result in a concrete object, such as a model of some science process or an artistic rendition of a historical event. The final product might be a report to the group on a field trip, or it could be an essay based entirely on library research supplemented with personal interpretations.

A project may be the stimulus for group discussion or the result of discussion. When an individual's project is presented, different interpretations will be volunteered from the class; some may question the way in which it was conducted while others may wish to develop the theme further. The individual responsible for the project then has the opportunity to reveal the results of his investigation into related areas. He is placed, in effect, in the role of a teacher and can explain to the others the rationale for his procedure. Whenever students can assume the role of teacher, the result is a beneficial increase in empathy for the role which can facilitate the teacher's task at other times. Many teachers fail to take advantage of opportunities for role-reversal and thus lose the chance to reduce the distance between teaching and learning. Perhaps the most effective way of all to learn a subject is to teach that subject. The nature of the preparation is different, and the desire to be ready for diverse questioning leads to more thorough understanding. Major research is needed to explore more fully the possibilities of casting students into the role of the teacher as a basic teaching method. Favorable changes in student's attitude toward the teaching-learning process would be a worth while result alone, but even more benefits can be reasonably expected.

RECITATION

Many people, especially older adults, think first of recitation when asked about their perception of classroom activity. For them, recitation, or *drill*, was the traditional practice and often the source of aversion toward school. When recitation, often perfunctory and preceded only by rote study, is the only classroom activity, the students soon become bored. Recitation can easily become meaningless, and without meaning there is reduced retention and, of course, little interest. The reactions of the students are barometers that should reveal to the weather eye of the teacher the moment when any one teaching technique has lost its efficiency through overuse.

SPECIALIZED TECHNIQUES

Psychologists have for a long time realized that the ideal way to learn how to function in an environment is to be placed in that environment. If an individual must live in another country where no one speaks his language, he quickly learns the new language in order to survive. The situation in a foreign language course is quite different. A student may be told he should learn certain material in order to receive a passing mark, but he often views the requirement as arbitrary at best or even as further persecution from the adult society. Even when motivation is high, what is learned often seems unrelated to the student's future. As we have seen earlier, high motivation may be the result of extrinsic incentives, e.g., grades, rather than intrinsic incentives such as the joy or utility of enlarged mastery. Often the reasons for having a student learn are not effective incentives for learning. The importance of being able to read cannot be used as direct motivation with a child in the first grade.

Outside of school, most learning is the result of movement toward an extrinsic rather than intrinsic goal. The goals are in the present, not in the distant future. The world of the present or very near future is the only world of the younger child; the ability to mediate between the present and the remote future is learned later. And many people never do learn to subordinate the lure of immediate gratification in order to achieve a greater reward tomorrow. The approval of a student's peers is often much more important to him than the approval of the teacher, who is frequently perceived as just one more adult authority. Part of the problem arises from the structure of education in our society. The teacher plays a dual role: one role is that of guiding the learning of students and giving them assistance with their problems, the second role, the source of student ambivalence, is that of judging performance, administering grades, and giving or withholding reinforcement. The attitudes that students develop toward teachers because of their role as judge and critic are often undesirable and may be manifested in many ways, from apathetic acquiescence to overt hostility.

SIMULATED ENVIRONMENTS

A considerable amount of effort has been directed toward the development of teaching techniques which simulate real social processes. These techniques are successful to the degree that they teach the content and skills that are needed for success in the world outside the classroom. To the extent that it is possible to produce a *simulated* environment (a realistic representation of a real problem area), the teacher can produce realistic learning about actual situations. If nothing is learned about the real process, then the simulation is not adequate. The use of war games by the military services to train men in decision making is an example: If what a soldier learns from a battle simulation is of no value in actual battle, the fault is probably not with him but with the simulation.

Simulations are also used in management training by many corporations and business schools. The player is given all the information he would normally have as an executive of a business firm, including the development of products, capital investment, marketing, and related problems. In some of these simulations, the student is playing against a computer which has been programed to behave as a representative economic environment. Realistic situations arise, and the student-player must make decisions, which are then evaluated by the computer. The consequences of any decision are fed back to the player, who may then modify his next move accordingly.

One goal of simulated environments is to bring the future into the present, to allow students to participate in roles which society would normally withhold for a very long time or roles they should understand even if they never will be in that role themselves,[2] e.g., governor of the state or president of a large corporation. In a simulation game, the student does not complete assignments but instead attempts to learn what he needs to cope with the environment in which he finds himself. In a management game, the student turns to economic texts not to earn a grade but to be successful in handling the simulated environment. Or, in a consumer game, the student must learn economics, mathematics, and the importance of deferring gratification because his simulated world includes credit financing, multiple attraction from competing products, and the realistic presence of unpredictable events.

In a legislative simulation, the students play the role of legislators who must gain support to pass some issues and defeat others. Each "legislator" starts with an electorate, knowing its sentiments on the relevant issues. If he is to be re-elected, he must please his hypothetical constituents by his record on the bills that are important to them. To gain support for an important issue, the legislator must be willing to make agreements with other legislators; that is, he must agree to support them on issues that are important to them but on which he is uncommitted in return for their support on issues that he deems important. After a time for discussion and argument, each issue is voted upon. More than one legislator can "win" because the game is structured so that it is possible for many players to use an adequate strategy. Not only is the game interesting to students, but it also teaches them the dependence of the legislator upon the electorate and other legislators. Some might say that the fact that legislators enter into "deals" with other legislators is an unfortunate aspect of our society and should not be simulated. However, this aspect of the simulation is realistic and can be used as a point for class discussion. Uninformed students will not become responsible citizens, and the schools have an obligation to present all facets of the important processes in our culture.

In another simulation—an election campaign game—students play the role of members of a campaign team competing to win votes for their candidate. Each team decides what position to take on a variety of national issues, which are then evaluated by a voting model. The voting model is based on a sample of real voters interviewed during a recent political campaign. There is, then, in a sense, a real electorate. Calculations during the game are done by a computer in which both the voting model and the data on the electorate are stored. The major activities of the game consist of studying and discussing the issues and deciding, with one's team-mates, which issues to present and how to present them. In later sessions of the game, the students are given survey materials which they can analyze for clues as to the kinds of campaign decisions which would lead to increases in votes.

The election campaign game is designed to teach the election process in a complex society by putting the student in the difficult position faced by actual candidates. Its purpose is not only to provide the student with specific information about national issues but also to give him the experience of playing a political role, an experience he would probably never have in real life. Also, the analysis of rather complicated survey materials and election returns gives the student valuable experience in handling complex problems systematically.

Simulations may also be used as part of a guidance program. In a college game, high school students make decisions about which courses to take in order to fulfill the requirements for college graduation. The college is hypothetical, but the degree requirements are realistic. The students decide how much time to allot for study and whether or not to participate in extracurricular activities. Grades are received from a schedule that empirically relates study time to success. In addition, situations arise that involve deciding whether to drop a course or to study more at the expense of some other activity.

The goal in the simulation is not only to graduate but to obtain employment or entrance into graduate school. The player must meet the requirements of the corporation or graduate school of his choice. These requirements may be some combination of both academic attainment and participation in extracurricular activities. The simulation teaches the importance of realistic time allotment for various college activities and the importance of completing basic requirements early in order to permit more flexible course scheduling later. Emphasis is placed on the goals that exist past college; graduation is not an end in itself. The simulation can be made even more realistic by the addition of other elements of college life—for example, the allocation of available financial resources for various purposes.

Simulated environments will need rigorous study as a teaching method before they can be adopted as part of the regular curriculum. There are many promising innovations at any given time in the history of education, but experience alone can reveal what is gold and what is only glitter.

TEACHING GAMES

Many techniques for producing learning rely on extrinsic rewards for engaging in an activity. Among these are a variety of games that is limited only by the imagination of the teacher. Many of these are used as a bonus activity for those students who successfully complete their regular assignment. At other times they may be used with the entire class in order to add variety to the more familiar activities. Realism is not a prime concern in these activities, although it is with simulations.

In a fishing game, children lower magnets on strings to catch paper fish (a paper clip attached to the fish is attracted by the magnet). If the child can read the word on the fish or give the answer to a number problem, he is allowed to keep the fish. Most students, especially younger ones, like activities that involve the physical manipulation of objects. There are also many puzzles designed to teach; the student must give correct responses to academic problems in order to complete the puzzle.

Other games involve teams. In a horse race game, if a team gives the correct response, its marker is advanced, and the team whose marker reaches the goal first is the winner. It is a mistake to assume that older students are not interested in similar activities. Often they will behave at first as though they are aloof to the playing of "games," but these activities can be surprisingly contagious and students who have previously shown little interest in anything occurring in the classroom may become involved.

In essence, there exists an endless array of activities that are fun and yet involve dealing with the very content that the teacher wants the students to learn. By no means should this be taken as a recommendation that the teacher should search for a candy-coating for all material worth learning. The point is simply that when an activity is enjoyed by students and is compatible with the values of education, it should be incorporated into the teaching-learning process.

PROGRAMED INSTRUCTION

Programed instruction may be regarded as a teaching method or as a medium for learning in the same sense as textbooks and workbooks. Viewed as a teaching technique, there is relatively little direct participation on the part of the teacher. The material to be learned is presented as short statements that usually terminate with a question or a blank to be filled in. The statements, or *frames*, may be presented by a *teaching machine* or by other methods. When the machine is used, the first statement appears in a window, where it can be read by the learner. If the first frame asks a question, the student writes his answer on a roll of paper which is exposed through another opening in the machine. Then the student makes the next frame appear (by pulling a lever or operating a roller); the correct response to the first frame appears together with the next frame. A sample of programed material on motivation might appear as follows:

Frame 1: We can define motivation in terms of goals. Whatever the individual is approaching through his activity may be called his _____.

Frame 2: *Goal*: The teacher wants students to reach certain goals. When students move toward a goal they are said to be motivated. Students will not move toward a goal if they are not _____.

Frame 3: *Motivated*: Sometimes people behave in a certain way because it will lead to one particular goal. In other cases a pattern of behavior may lead to several _____.

Frame 4: *Goals*: Goals differ in many ways. People want and approach some goals because they are more attractive than others. The goals that are the most attractive are the ones that people will _____.

Frame 5: *Want, Approach*: If people do not approach a goal, it may be because some other goal is more _____.

In this type of program the necessary information for a correct response is provided in the text of the frames. Each statement is worded so as to lead in a line to the next; for this reason, the program is called *linear*.

The main advantages claimed for programed instruction are the immediate feedback provided to the learner and the fact that each learner determines his own rate of progress. The bright student can proceed rapidly and be given more difficult material, whereas the slower individual can find the pace that is most comfortable for him. It is argued that since the correct responses are incorporated in the frames, learning should proceed without error, thus resulting in a very positive attitude toward learning. In practice, this is not always true. The linear program fails to make adequate provision for confusion. However, the program tries to avoid this confusion by supplying a high degree of redundancy: each item of new material is presented several times. The learner has repeated opportunities to get the point, but this same redundancy can be rather boring to the more talented individual.

One attempt to avoid the limitations of linear programing is through the use of a *branching* format. When the program is presented in a text, the student reads a selection which is followed by a multiple-choice question. When he makes his selection, he is referred to another page. His choice determines which page he is referred to. If he is correct, he is so informed and further material is presented. A wrong answer leads him to a page that explains why he is in error and directs him to the correct solution. This technique has the advantage that the wrong answers can be designed to pick up the most probable forms of confusion and set the learner on the right path. Unlike the linear program, where the student must *construct* answers, the branching program usually requires only that he be able to *recognize* the correct answer. With the branching program the able student will proceed directly through the program without enduring redundancy. The slower student, on the other hand, takes a more circuitous route to the same goal. He enjoys the redundancy which he requires, a degree of repetition that the teacher would not want to provide for the entire class.

As we have already mentioned, programed material can be presented by a teaching machine or in a textbook by placing successive frames on successive pages.

A third method of presenting programed material is through the use of a computer. In one experimental version, the student makes his responses on an electric typewriter that is "slaved" to the computer. The computer then prints out new material as determined by the quality of the student's reply. The computer can be programed to evaluate the nature of an incorrect response and present what is appropriate for further instruction. The computer can evaluate and respond to the performance of many students simultaneously.

Besides providing the learner with immediate feedback and allowing him to determine his own rate of progress, programed instruction takes the teacher out of the role of giving and withholding reinforcement during the learning process. The reinforcement is provided by the knowledge that one's response is correct. Parenthetically, it should be noted that flash cards, a very effective study device for some material, also have the feature of immediate feedback and self-reinforcement.

There is one valuable advantage of programing in addition to those already mentioned. To program a subject, it is necessary to organize its content in a way not required in a lecture or general textbook. The programer must decide what is most important for the students to learn. By including a particular item in the program, he makes this value judgment. The decisions about what should be learned and the organization of subject matter forced by the task of programing may be incorporated into other teaching methods at some later time.

The role that will be played by the various forms of programed instruction in education has not yet been determined and probably will not be for some time. It may become a major method of instruction or a minor supplement to other methods, perhaps as a form of enrichment. Only research and the reactions of teachers and students will provide the final answer. It is no simple matter to conduct adequate research that compares programed instruction with other techniques because it differs in so many ways. In addition to novelty effects, there is the problem that programed instruction is based on students working alone, whereas other methods are centered on groups. But perhaps one of the greatest differences is that a program is the result of many hours of painstaking effort for perfect wording and organization. If the same amount of time were put into producing a perfect lecture or discussion session, these time-honored techniques would be vastly improved.

CHOOSING A TEACHING METHOD

We have discussed how various teaching techniques attempt to cope with the most fundamental problems of instruction. These considerations include:

1. Directing the student's attention to the specific nature of the learning task so that he will know exactly what is expected of him.
2. Providing for or arousing motivation to learn.
3. Maintaining interest.
4. Providing immediate feedback.
5. Allowing student to progress at his own rate.
6. Avoiding excessive frustration and failure.
7. Promoting transfer of learning to situations outside of the classroom.
8. Developing and preserving positive attitudes toward self, the teacher, the subject matter, and the education process in general.

The special techniques differ in their virtues. Simulations arouse interest and provide for transfer, but they often do not direct attention to the specific elements that must be learned. The student must discover what is important and what is not. Teaching games promote high motivation, and it is clear what must be learned. One must spell the word correctly or know the right answer in order to earn points for himself or his team. There is, however, little provision for transfer. Programed instruction makes it quite clear what is to be learned, and each student can advance at his own rate, but the questions of transfer and long-term maintenance of interest seem to be unanswered. Any one teaching method will have its defects as well as its virtues. For this reason the successful teacher will vary his approach in accordance with the problems that arise as well as for variety itself.

The ways in which an individual was taught have a strong influence on the methods he will choose when he himself becomes a teacher. Practice teaching and the observation of other teachers—part of most college programs leading to an education degree—also shape the classroom behavior of the new teacher. The prevalent methods used differ from one culture to another and reflect the values of the culture in which they occur. Schools also differ from one another in the teaching atmosphere that prevails. A new teacher tends to acquire the practices and conventions of those teachers who have been at the school for a long time.

The forces of tradition make it quite difficult to introduce new teaching methods. Besides the inertia of existing methods, there is the problem of avoiding threat to teachers using the traditional approach. It is understandable that experienced teachers will resist change if they are made to feel that the way they have been teaching is inferior or that they must learn new skills. They will insist that the old way is the best way and find fault with the innovation. If the new teacher is aware of the understandable concern of other teachers over *their* way of teaching, he can prevent conflict through the use of reasonable restraint and common sense. Most professions, including teaching, tend to be conservative institutions. It is apparent why this should be so: a profession is based on learned skills, and when these skills become obsolete and new ones must be learned, the security of the professional, if not of the profession itself, is at stake.

The traditional methods have withstood the test of time. They do work or they would have been rejected long ago. A new method may be superior, but this must be demonstrated before old ways are abandoned, and it takes time for a new method to prove itself and win acceptance. In some parts of our culture, there is a tendency to assume that whatever is new is also the best. In education, this predilection must be guarded against until the new concept has been properly evaluated.

Techniques that are now traditional were, of course, at one time new. And, naturally, no teaching method has failed to undergo subtle changes in response to changing values of the culture. Some teaching methods are the result of philosophies of education that are based on specific theories of man and that possess a definite value system. For example, the Socratic method is based on the theory that the individual already possesses all knowledge and that the task of the teacher is to guide him to the point of rediscovery. This is done by questioning the student until he comes to certain conclusions as the result of his own answers to astute inquiry. Whether or not a teaching method promotes learning is a separate question from the validity of the premises on which it is based. Philosophies of education may produce a value system rather than a specific method, but only methods that are compatible with the value system will be adopted. Rousseau and Froebel have exerted a pervasive influence upon the values of education in this country. The notion that the child should develop naturally and will do so if given the correct environment is central to the system. Instead of interfering with the natural process, one must recognize each individual as having individual worth and give him freedom to grow. Some educators interpreted this doctrine as being very permissive, while others were more moderate in their appraisal. Rather than yielding explicit teaching methods, the various philosophies presented certain values against which teaching methods were tested. Methods compatible with the values were accepted and others were rejected.

Teaching methods can result from systematic research on different ways of teaching the same material. Or, the research can stem from a particular theory of learning. In general, though, theories of learning have seldom resulted in attempts to experiment with methods of teaching which derive from the theories. As was suggested earlier, formal learning theory has more to say about why learning occurs than it does about the facilitation of the process.

It is possible to conduct research on teaching methods without deriving hypotheses from a formal theory. By observation in the classroom, an investigator may form the hypothesis that a particular method would be more effective than existing techniques. Proper research may reveal that it is, in fact, a superior method. If the forces of tradition can be overcome, the new method may become part of standard teaching practice.

There are other factors that determine which teaching methods are employed in a given situation. One school system may have a philosophy of social reconstruction the goal of which is to instill in students values lacking in society now in order that the society of tomorrow will be different in that respect. Another school system may hold the philosophy that the function of formal education is to transmit the existing culture rather than strive for change. These two school systems may use different methods in an attempt to reach the goals that are a part of their value scheme.

Within a school, different teachers, because of their unique personalities, prefer different methods. One teacher is most comfortable, and most effective, using a teaching method that would present considerable problems for another teacher. Also, children of different ages or in special classes require different methods. A class of predominantly gifted students can be taught with methods that could not be employed with a class of slow learners.

Mixed teaching methods will probably always be superior to any one method given as a steady dose. One method may be the best at a given moment but not a short time later. The personalities of both teachers and students, combined with their changing interests, will determine what is most effective for learning at the moment. The teacher must make use of subjective factors in many teaching decisions; there is no formula for the benefit of the inexperienced.

If the students are learning what they should at a level near to their capacity, the teaching method is probably a good one. When this is the case, other tests of the adequacy of the method are the attitudes of the learners (usually revealed by the degree of enthusiasm evoked) and the extent to which transfer of learning occurs. When the results fall short of this ideal, the teacher should modify or completely change his method of teaching. The exact nature of the required change will be determined by the specific problem. Again, there is no one best teaching method; the teacher must be willing to experiment and perhaps experiment often. Teaching requires a capacity for tolerating ambiguity, but it is still quite natural for the teacher to want some guidelines to follow.

In Table VI.I, the different forms of teaching discussed so far are judged on the eight fundamental requirements of a good teaching technique presented on page 140. The ratings are based on the previous discussion of the different methods as well as earlier consideration of the psychology of learning and motivation. Naturally, a superior teacher could, in many instances, overcome the limitations of a particular technique, and a poor teacher might fail to capitalize on the advantages of any form of instruction. The ratings are intended, then, to reflect advantages and defects inherent in the method rather than in the teacher.

NEW WAYS OF ORGANIZING TEACHERS AND STUDENTS

TEAM TEACHING

In team teaching, more than one teacher is involved in the teaching of the same students. This approach may assume an endless number of forms. The team may consist of only two teachers or it may be a much larger group, containing specialists in

TABLE VI.1

	Directs Attention	Promotes Motivation	Maintains Interest	Provides Immediate Feedback	Allows Student to Progress at His Own Rate	Avoids Excessive Frustration and Failure	Promotes Transfer	Develops Positive Attitudes
Discussion	Usually	Usually	Usually	Yes	Usually	Usually	Usually	Usually
Games	Does, but indirectly	Usually	Usually	Yes	Usually	Often does not	Seldom	Usually
Lecture	Can, with a little effort	Can, but often fails to	Can, but often fails to	No	Rarely	Usually	Rarely does without special care	Can, if interesting
Programed Instruction	Almost always	Does, at least in beginning	Depends on material	Yes	Yes	Usually	Usually does not	Uncertain
Projects	Usually	Usually	Usually	Yes, when projects or parts of it are completed	Usually	Often does not	Often does not	Does, if project is successful
Recitation or Drill	Always	Rarely	Rarely	Yes, when oral No, when written	Usually, but not for better students	Rarely	Rarely, if ever	Rarely, if ever
Simulations	Often does not	Usually	Usually	Usually, depending on specific simulation	Usually	If well designed	Always, if simulation is adequate	In majority of cases

specific subjects and, perhaps, in guidance and other services. More complex structures of team teaching can have, in addition, visits from experts who are not connected with the school—coordinating specialists, clerical aids, and a variety of other adjunct personnel.

One advantage of team teaching is that when students have more than one teacher in the same span of time, the teaching methods are more likely to vary. Also, exposure to different personalities can make the day more interesting. After the sixth grade, students usually have different teachers during the day, but this is not the same as team teaching, where there is some degree of coordination of the teaching tasks. When teachers know what is being taught to their students by other teachers, they can make their own teaching more meaningful by relating it to the other subjects. Special problems of students can also receive more effective consideration when there is a channel of communication between the teachers. Without this provision, a teacher may be unaware of a very serious problem because his contact with each student is relatively brief.

In the simplest form of team teaching, teachers go into each other's class when their specialty permits them to make a unique contribution. A biologist could lead an interesting discussion of the role various chemical processes play in human lives if he visited a chemistry class that was studying organic compounds. A teacher of Latin could provide interesting insights into the origin of words for the benefit of an English class. It has been said that "the cloak of knowledge is seamless"; perhaps the interrelationship of the various disciplines can be brought home to students through this form of team teaching.

NONGRADED CLASSROOMS AND HOUSE SYSTEMS

There are other ways to arrange students and teachers than the conventional pattern and the team-teaching system. The *nongraded* school allows for the fact that a child in any given year of elementary school may be below that level in some areas or above that level in others. A nine-year-old student might take reading with a group that averages eight years of age and arithmetic with a group that averages ten. The aim of this plan is to avoid the conventional situation where this student would automatically be placed in the fourth grade, frustrated by the reading level and bored by the arithmetic level of that grade.

Another way of organizing students and teachers is *house systems*, where a very large high school with thousands of students is divided into "houses" of a few hundred students, each with their own faculty and director. The advantage is that all of the houses can share the same cafeteria, gymnasium, and other facilities while enjoying sufficiently small size to promote feelings of individuality and identification.

Just as there is no one best teaching method, so there is probably no one best way of organizing the formal structure of the school, because specific situations differ so much in their requirements. Continuing investigations of this topic should reveal the effects of the interaction between different school structures, age of students, and various social and academic parameters.

STYLES OF TEACHING

Although it is often forgotten, teachers *are people*. And, of course, so are students. When a person becomes a teacher, he does not lose that unique combination of personality traits and attitudes which make an individual different to some extent from everyone else. The interaction between a particular teacher and student in the teaching-learning process can involve all the complexities of interpersonal dynamics that characterize all human encounters. Obviously, we cannot explore in depth all of the dimensions of personality that could be relevant to the teacher's performance, but a few traits are worth discussing because they are often a source of difficulty. For the teacher, or prospective teacher, to recognize that he has some of these tendencies is half of the battle. Self-scrutiny can often provide sufficient insight so that the individual can make some allowances for his predilections which will permit him to function more adequately as a teacher and as a person in general.

Specific prejudices based on race, religion, or sex can result in biased reactions to individual students. Ideally these prejudices should not exist, but they do, and, often, ignoring the problem will not change the real world. When a teacher finds himself reacting to certain students in a manner not explicable in terms of the actual situation, he must examine his own motives and attitudes. If the teacher is prepared to do this, he is much less likely to allow any injustices to be perpetuated. When a student does better or worse on objective tests than he does on material that requires a subjective grade from the teacher, there may be a possibility that something is amiss. It could simply be that the student really does perform at different levels on different types of tests, but it could be that the subjective decisions of the teacher are influenced by factors unrelated to the level of achievement demonstrated in the examination. For example, it has been shown that teachers tend to give girls higher grades and boys lower grades than they actually deserve. This bias has been attributed to the difference in conduct between boys and girls which leads the teacher to perceive the girls as better students than the boys.

The way in which the teacher handles authority can be significant. Teachers who are insecure about their authority will often overreact to behavior that seems to threaten their control. When the teacher recalls the fundamental distinction between his role and the role of the student, he will be able to cope with this behavior in a more rational way. In turn, the teacher must be able to accept the authority of the principal and supervisors. Those who know that they have trouble interacting with people in positions of authority must learn to avoid resenting all suggestions or directives. However, to feel injured by an unjust criticism is quite a different matter from a reaction based on its source independently of its merit. It is true that some people in positions of authority make suggestions tactlessly, but these people will be encountered in any occupation. What cannot be ignored must often be endured, and need not be taken personally.

Just as some teachers are too rigid in their control of the classroom, others are too permissive or acquiescent. Sometimes this results from a desire to be popular with the students, to be liked by them. But it usually does not work that way. Students, especially younger ones, want to know what the rules are; they find security in the knowledge of what is permissible and what is not. Children will test the limits in an effort to discover how they should behave, both at home and in the classroom. When they fail to find the limits, they go right on testing in ways that become increasingly extreme. By allowing his students to push him around, a teacher loses rather than gains popularity and the respect of his students. On the other hand, fairness and the avoidance of unequal treatment lead to both respect and popularity.

A frequent source of unequal treatment in the elementary school is what might be called "the need to mother." Some women who teach young children will adopt very maternal attitudes toward certain children because of their own unsatisfied needs. This always leads to the creation of favorites, who may be embarrassed, and outcasts, who are resentful that they are rejected. Also, some children, because of an unfortunate home situation, have a strong need to be mothered and are easily led into a relationship with the teacher that satisfies them for the time but is in the long run detrimental to all concerned. The teacher who finds that he likes some students much more than others should engage in a little introspection to answer the question "Why?" Other normal emotions of the teacher that can give rise to difficulties include aggression, hostility, and anxiety, which can occur when students do not react in the way he wishes or when they themselves reveal hostility and defiance. It is quite normal for the teacher to feel all these emotions and many others in certain situation, but they should not be allowed to interfere with the teaching-learning process.

Many studies have been conducted to discover those personality characteristics and attitudes that are typical of the successful teacher but lacking in those who are less effective. The results are not surprising. Instead of some subtle facets of complex dynamics, the obvious traits emerge that allow anyone to be effective in sustained social interaction. Successful teachers, as judged by their colleagues, are warm, friendly, empathetic, and display the sense of humor typical of any cheerful person.[3] When these attributes are absent, a definite handicap exists to the perpetuation of any social process, including teaching.

Because both students and teachers have varied personalities, a teacher may work well with one student and not another, or a student may respond to one teacher and not another. The teacher can be most effective when he knows as much as possible about each member of the class, including his home situation. In one very deprived neighborhood, a teacher had the children read a page of their reader to their parents each evening as part of their homework. She stopped this practice when she discovered that several of the children were physically punished for their lack of proficiency. Without this knowledge, the teacher could have easily misinterpreted the attitude of these children toward home assignments. This is only one example of the many conflicts that can result when there is a significant difference between the cultural environment of the students and that of the teacher, and the teacher fails to realize that the difference exists. The *child study* movement has been based primarily on recognition of the importance of knowing as much as possible about the learner, including his learning ability, motivation, interests, personality, attitudes, and cultural orientation.

In this chapter, as in the preceding ones, we have examined some of the myriad variables that play a role in the teaching-learning process. Some of the factors are essentially properties of the student: they have to do with the nature of learning as determined by empirical studies of the possibility of modifying human behavior and thinking by experience. Most of the *principles* of learning could be placed here. Other learner variables included age, sex, interests, attitudes, and personality. Teaching methods and styles might be regarded as primarily teacher variables. Some factors could be considered intrinsic to the content of what is to be learned. However, as far as the teaching-learning process is concerned, such categorization of variables is probably not only arbitrary but completely misleading. The process of education is influenced by the interaction of all these elements. The complexity of the interaction and the unique aspects of any given interaction make it impossible to generate general statements about how to teach or the "best" way to teach. An effective technique will usually work because it meets the requirements of a very specific situation. A different situation will vary in at least a few of the many components we have considered. As was discussed in Chapter Two, some principles of education do have considerable generality, but this is not true of many of the techniques that can be used to implement those principles. The choice of the right technique requires a combination of common sense and a basic understanding of the foundations of the teaching-learning process. The teacher who cares about the critical role that he is performing in our society will be ready to give the necessary thought and effort that is required to be a superior teacher.

FOOTNOTES

INTRODUCTION
1. *Foundations of Method* (New York: The Macmillan Company, 1925), p. 268.
2. *How We Think* (Boston: D. C. Heath & Company, 1933), pp. 35-36.
3. J. L. Kuethe, "Education: The Discipline That Concern Built," an essay in *The Discipline of Education,* eds. J. Walton and J. L. Kuethe (Madison: University of Wisconsin Press, 1963).

CHAPTER ONE
1. H. Head, *Studies in Neurology* (New York: Oxford University Press, 1920), p. 605.
2. F. C. Bartlett, *Remembering* (Cambridge, England: Cambridge University Press, 1932), p. 201.
3. *Ibid.,* pp. 207-208.
4. *Ibid.,* p. 202.
5. John B. Watson, *The Ways of Behaviorism* (New York: Harper and Bros., 1928), p. 3.
6. Psychologists also measure an increase in the strength of response by its magnitude and its latency. Additional reinforcements cause the response to have greater amplitude and to occur more quickly as well as more frequently.
7. See H. F. Harlow and J. M. Warren, "Formation and Transfer of Discrimination Learning Sets," *Journal of Comparative Physiological Psychology,* XLV (1952), 482-489.
8. See E. H. Hess, "Imprinting," *Science,* CXXX (1959), 133-141.

CHAPTER THREE
1. "Value and Need as Organizing Factors in Perception," *Journal of Abnormal Social Psychology,* XLII (1947), 33-34.

2. J. L. Kuethe, "The Acquiescence Response Set and the Psychasthenia Scale: An Analysis via the 'Aussage' Experiment," *Journal of Abnormal Social Psychology,* LXI (1960), 319-322.
3. J. L. Kuethe, "Social Schema," *Journal of Abnormal Social Psychology,* LXIV (1962), 31-38.
4. J. L. Kuethe, "Pervasive Influence of Social Schemata," *Journal of Abnormal Social Psychology,* LXVIII (1964), 248-254.
5. See B. Zeigarnik, "Über das Behalten von erledigten und unerledigten Handlungen," *Psychologische Forschung,* IX (1927), 1-85.
6. See P. Rosenzweig, "Need-Persistive and Ego-Defensive Reactions to Frustration as Demonstrated by an Experiment on Repression," *Psychological Review,* XLVIII (1941), 347-349.
7. "The Associative Structure of Schemata in Science and Their Relationship to Problem Solving Behavior." (Ph.D. dissertation at the Johns Hopkins University, 1964).

CHAPTER FOUR
1. William James, *Talks to Teachers on Psychology and to Students on Some of Life's Ideals* (New York: Henry Holt and Co., 1899), p. 150.
2. J. L. Kuethe, "The Retention of Science Concepts: A Study of 'Sophisticated' Errors," *Science Education,* XLVII (1963), 361-364.
3. K. Duncker, "On Problem Solving," *Psychological Monographs,* LVIII, No. 5 (1945), 86.

CHAPTER FIVE
1. The reader who wishes to pursue the concepts presented in this section should refer to N. E. Miller, "Experimental Studies in

Conflict," in *Personality and the Behavior Disorders*, ed. J. McV. Hunt, Vol. I (New York: The Ronald Press Company, 1944).

2. D. C. McClelland, J. W. Atkinson, R. A. Clark, and E. L. Lowell, *The Achievement Motive* (New York: Appleton-Century-Crofts, 1953).

3. See A. H. Maslow, "Self-Actualizing People: A Study of Psychological Health," in *Personality Symposium*, ed. W. Wolf, No. 1 (New York: Grune & Stratton, Inc., 1950).

CHAPTER SIX
1. From the Latin *legere* meaning "to read."

2. Several of the simulations presented in the following discussion were initiated by a grant from the Carnegie Corporation of New York to James S. Coleman and James L. Kuethe.

3. See D. G. Ryans, *Characteristics of Teachers: Their Description, Comparison and Appraisal* (Washington, D.C.: American Council on Education, 1960).

BIBLIOGRAPHY

There are a number of valuable sources in addition to those specifically cited in the preceding text. Some of these are suggested below; other topics may be pursued in Chester W. Harris, ed. *Encyclopedia of Educational Research,* 3rd ed. (New York: The Macmillan Company, 1960) and *Psychological Abstracts,* published by the American Psychological Association.

INTRODUCTION

The various problems that arise from attempts to define learning are given an excellent treatment by Kimble. Those interested in the topic of *response sets* are referred to the classic study by Cronbach. Anderson is one of many authors who are concerned with development and the question of early sex differences in the performance of children. The books by Breckenridge and Murphy, and Mussen's *Handbook* present important data on this topic.

Anderson, John E. *The Psychology of Development and Personal Adjustment.* New York, Henry Holt and Co., 1949.
Breckenridge, Marian E. and Margaret N. Murphy. *Growth and Development of the Young Child.* Philadelphia, W. B. Saunders Co., 1963.
Cronbach, L. J. "Response Sets and Test Validity," *Educational and Psychological Measurement,* VI (1946), 475-494.
Kimble, George A. *Hilgard and Marquis' Conditioning and Learning.* New York, Appleton-Century-Crofts, 1961, Chapter I.
Mussen, P. H., ed. *Handbook of Research Methods in Child Development.* New York, John Wiley and Sons, Inc., 1960.

CHAPTER ONE

A full treatment of the history of associationism and learning theories is given by Boring and by Brett. A general discussion of the various learning theories and special problems in learning may be found in the books by Deese and by Bugelski which provide a broad general treatment of the psychology of learning as does the text by McGeoch and Irion.

Boring, E. G. *A History of Experimental Psychology.* 2nd ed. New York, Appleton-Century-Crofts, 1950.
Brett, G. S. *A History of Psychology.* New York, The Macmillan Company, 1921.
Bugelski, B. R. *The Psychology of Learning.* New York, Holt, Rinehart & Winston, Inc., 1958.
Deese, J. E. *The Psychology of Learning.* New York, McGraw-Hill Book Company, Inc., 1958.
McGeoch, J. A., and A. L. Irion. *The Psychology of Human Learning.* Revised ed. New York, David McKay Company Inc., 1952.

CHAPTER TWO

Scholars from the fields of education, psychology, sociology, history, and philosophy answer the question "Is education a discipline in the sense of the traditional academic disciplines?" in a volume edited by Walton and Kuethe.

Walton, J., and Kuethe, J. L. *The Discipline of Education.* Madison, The University of Wisconsin Press, 1963.

CHAPTER THREE

Discussion of the various reinforcement schedules may be found in the general psychology of learning texts suggested in the bibliography for Chapter One. Most general texts also provide treatments of memory, forgetting, and the concept of interference. Underwood's article on forgetting is a more specific source. Thorndike's treatment of the concepts of achievement and under-achievement is useful. Bartlett's work is required reading on some of the factors that produce distortion of recall. Other specific topics (e.g., social schemata) are referenced in the text of Chapter Three.

Bartlett, F. C. *Remembering*. Cambridge, England, Cambridge University Press, 1932.

Thorndike, Robert L. *The Concepts of Over- and Underachievement*. New York, Bureau of Publications, Teachers College, Columbia University, 1963.

Underwood, B. J. "Forgetting," *Scientific American*, CCX, No. 3 (March 1964), 91-99.

CHAPTER FOUR

A different way of regarding meaningfulness and its measurement may be found in Osgood. Also, the book by Ausubel should be of use to the educator and he might review the work of Underwood and Schulz. Creativity and its assessment is considered in depth by Getzels and Jackson as well as by other writers.

Ausubel, D. P. *The Psychology of Meaningful Verbal Learning; an Introduction to School Learning*. New York, Grune and Stratton, Inc., 1963.

Getzels, J. W., and P. W. Jackson. *Creativity and Intelligence, Explorations with Gifted Students*. New York, John Wiley & Sons, Inc., 1962.

Osgood, C. E., G. J. Suci, and Tannenbaum. *The Measurement of Meaning*. Urbana, Illinois, University of Illinois Press, 1957.

Underwood, B. J., and R. W. Schulz. *Meaningfulness and Verbal Learning*. Philadelphia, J. B. Lippincott Company, 1960.

CHAPTER FIVE

McClelland and others discuss the achievement motive and its relation to personality and to various demographic variables. The work of Miller on the conflict of motives is basic. Other suggestions for further reading on motivation are listed below. The attitudes of the adolescent which affect his motivation for academic performance are investigated by Coleman in the context of an "adolescent society."

Coleman, J. S. *The Adolescent Society; the Social Life of the Teenager and Its Impact on Education*. New York, Free Press of Glencoe, 1961.

Brown, J. S. *Motivation of Behavior*. New York, McGraw-Hill, Inc., 1961.

Miller, N. E. "Experimental Studies of Conflict," in *Personality and the Behavior Disorders*, ed. J. McV. Hunt. New York, The Ronald Press Company, I (1944), 431-465.

McClelland, D. C., J. W. Atkinson, R. A. Clark, and E. L. Lowell. *The Achievement Motive*. New York, Appleton-Century-Crofts, 1953.

Sears, Pauline S., and E. R. Hilgard. "The Teacher's Role in the Motivation of the Learner,"

Yearbook National Society for the Study of Education, LXIII, pt. 1 (1964), 182-209.

CHAPTER SIX

Those interested in methods of teaching, teaching characteristics, and many other topics which were previously discussed, should consult Gage's *Handbook of Research on Teaching*. Gabriel's consideration of the teacher's emotional problems is one treatment of a critical problem as is the article by Witty. On programed instruction and teaching machines see, for example, Fry or Silberman, as well as Skinner. Guetzkow has edited a collection of papers concerning the use of simulations in various areas, including education. One collection of papers, edited by Shaplin, presents several views of team teaching.

Fry, E. B. *Teaching Machines and Programmed Instruction, an Introduction*. New York, McGraw-Hill, Inc., 1963.

Gabriel, J. *An Analysis of the Emotional Problems of the Teacher in the Classroom*. Melbourne, F. W. Cheshire, Publishers, 1957.

Gage, N. L., ed. *Handbook of Research on Teaching*. Chicago, Rand McNally, 1963.

Guetzkow, H., ed. *Simulation in Social Science: Readings*. Englewood Cliffs, N.J., Prentice-Hall, Inc., 1962.

Shaplin, J. T., ed. *Team Teaching*. New York, Harper & Row, 1964.

Silberman, H. F. "Self-teaching Devices and Programmed Materials," *Review of Educational Research*, XXXII (1962), 179-193.

Skinner, B. F. "Teaching Machines," *Science*, CXXVIII (October 1958), 969-977.

Witty, P. A., "Mental Health of the Teacher," *Yearbook National Society for the Study of Education*, LIV, pt. 2 (1955), 307-333.

INDEX

A